Dedicated to my longtime friend and intercessor Mike Grant.

He is now with Jesus, having pioneered two Houses of Prayer.

When an awakening finally arrives, it will be in part due to your

many years of life and death prayers for Heaven to come to Earth.

I love you and miss you, my dear friend.

The Rock of Roseville
725 Vernon St., Roseville, CA
95678 U.S.A.

www.rockofroseville.com

Copyright © 2012 The Rock of Roseville.

Cover design & book layout by Hans Bennewitz

Unless otherwise indicated, all Scripture quotations are taken from
the Holy Bible, copyright © 1996, 2004, 2007 by the Tyndale House
Foundation. Used by permission of Tyndale House Publishers, Inc.,
Carol Stream, Illinois 60188. All rights reserved.

ISBN:978-1-936417-87-2

AWAKENED.
FRANCIS ANFUSO

One-hour video may be viewed at:

www.revivalstories.org/awakened

FOREWORD

For more than three decades it has been my honor to know and deeply appreciate my friend in the faith who is the author of this small book. He is a man who through his other writings and speaking gifts, by evangelistic and counseling materials with visual and audio communications to both the church and the street, has constantly sought for all of us one thing; a fresh visitation in our day of the Living God.

Francis is a creative exhorter. His solid biblical studies, succinct insights from recorded history by analysis of the words and lives of passionate prophets and truth-seeking people of the past have always carried a core mission. It has marked all of his work. It is the goal of this book. And we need it now more than ever before.

What is this book about? To take key DNA of a special spiritual past and restore it again in our needy present to see Christ create a new future. To help the Church rediscover a path to an awakened present in the hope of having another Divine mercy chance for the nation.

In summary: to see again a God-given genuine revival.

I believe Awakened can and will prove for many to be one of the most useful, practical contemporary series of studies in one of the most needed and significant focuses of our time.

Winkie Pratney: June 2012
(Revival; Twenty Centuries of Vision and Visitation,
The Revival Study Bible)

ACKNOWLEDGMENTS

I have at times thought my tombstone might read, "He persecuted the Church," due to what I ask others around me to do, and when I ask them to do it. My mind is always active, schedule brisk, and timeframes for completing projects often taxing. Though I may willingly submit my life to what some call this "Tyranny of the Urgent," I often feel sad for those who have to ski in my wake. In the past, my leaving town would provide a needed respite. That is, until the marvelous inventions: email and texting.

So, the least I can do is express my sincerest appreciation to the mighty warriors who help me fulfill what I believe is God's script for my life. May eternity reward your willingness and obedience, and may you find more margin in the present than I am aware of.

Suzie, my beautiful and wise wife, what I lack in patience you model every day. Lydia, you have been a faithful and flexible assistant for many years. Stephanie, thanks for helping me structure this book. Kathy, you are a perfect and selfless editor for my many books. Betty, you're brilliant in making sure every detail and footnote is precise. Adena, thanks for jumping in and refining the chapters' questions. John, your coaching me for the final section was a difference-maker. Hans, "Mr. No Problem," you always make the book, inside and out, exquisite.

Sean, your book, "I Am Your Sign" gave me a new gear of hope for the future. Winkie, years ago you jumpstarted my understanding of revival with your book, Revival. Now, you've added fuel to my fire with, The Revival Study Bible. Thanks for your supportive Foreword, and being a bright light all these years.

Joel, I loved filming with you in Wales, and watching your creativity flow. Ben, your music gave the film the warmth and heart it needed. Dick and Gladys, you received us into your home and guided us as we traversed your beautiful adopted nation: Wales. Intercessors, only Heaven will reveal how your prayers bolstered and protected me throughout the writing and filming of this project. Interns, your all night prayer made the difference. God knows! My children and grandchildren, your future inspires me to believe for a global awakening. Jesus, You are the One I live for, love most, and long to see face to face.

Francis Anfuso

INTRODUCTION

The Holy Spirit has made it exceedingly clear to me that unless there is a mighty move of God in America, the Church cannot be revived, nor the lost awakened. The Church is not ready. Not unless we pray and obediently believe for a revival of His Spirit.

Shortly after I received this distinct impression, I went away to a retreat center for three days to pray and fast. During that time of focused reflection I reread many of the books on revival and the biographies of great evangelists and intercessors who had inspired me during my 40 years of following Jesus.

I came to the following two conclusions:

1. Though revival is a supernatural act of God, and not contrived in any way, there are clear Biblical and historical dimensions that we can obediently pursue in preparation for God to revive the Church before awakening the lost.

2. Commitment to step into these areas requires full surrender and whole-hearted abandon to Jesus.

3. The greatest revivals in Church History were filled with grave dangers before, during, and after the moving of God's Spirit.

This book was written to rekindle our passion for Jesus while preparing us for the sovereign outpouring we so desperately need. May we each find our unique role for all that is ahead and be fully protected during the ensuing battle.

In the book, *The Ten Greatest Revivals Ever*, the authors list in order the historic revivals that had the greatest impact.[1,2]

1. Revival of 1904–1906 (*Welsh and Azusa Street Revivals*)

2. Great Awakening, 1727–1750 (*Wesley, Whitefield, Edwards*)

3. Second Great Awakening, 1780–1810 (*Cane Ridge Revival*)

4. General Awakening, 1830–1840 (*Charles Finney*)

5. Layman's Prayer Revival, 1857–1861 (*Lanphier, Moody*)

1   Towns EL. *The Ten Greatest Revivals Ever.* Servant Publications: Ann Arbor, MI; 2000 (out of print).
2   The order of the Ten Greatest Revivals Ever...Complete footnote: francisanfuso.com/awakened

6. World War II Revival, 1935–1950 (*Graham, Campbell*)

7. Baby Boomer Revival, 1965–1975 (*Jesus People*)

8. Pre-Reformation Revivals, 1300–1500
   (*Lollards, Wycliffe, Hus, Savonarola*)

9. Protestant Reformation, 1517 (*Luther, Calvin, Zwingli, Knox*)

10. Pentecost, the Beginning of Revival, A.D. 30 (*Peter and Paul*)

In each of these ten periods of awakening, the expressions of revival appeared differently. The most common demonstrations of God moving are described as "nine faces of revival" and are listed in the book, *Rivers of Revival*.[3] While most revivals demonstrated a cross section of these historic faces, as the revival spread, individual locales tended to focus on one predominant face.

1. *Prayer Revival:* movement of intercession and prayer.

2. *Repentance Revival:* stresses cleaning up one's life and society.

3. *Worship Revival:* emphasis on magnifying God's presence.

4. *Liberation Revival:* God's Word and freedom from sin.

5. *Deeper Life Revival:* experiencing God's indwelling Spirit.

6. *Reconciliation Revival:* healing racial and relational divisions.

7. *Evangelism Revival:* God's servant heart rescuing the lost.

8. *Holy Spirit Revival:* emphasis on the Spirit's manifestations.

9. *Spiritual Warfare Revival:* victory over powers of darkness.

Though we have not compartmentalized our chapters in the above-mentioned format, these faces of revival are seen throughout this book. It is our hope that they will once again permeate each of our lives, being part of the great birthing process for the next great awakening.

In closing, the following quote aptly describes how God interrupts our mundane lives and transforms a community. It was written by Jonathan Edwards and recounts how God touched the little town of Northampton, Massachusetts in 1734–1735.

---

3 Towns E, Anderson N. *Rivers of Revival*. Regal Books; 1998.

This work soon made a glorious alteration in the town. So that in the spring and summer following, the town seemed to be full of the presence of God. It never was so full of love nor so full of joy and yet so full of distress as it was then.

There were remarkable tokens of God's presence in almost every house. It was a time of joy in families on account of salvation being brought to them. Parents rejoicing over their children as newborn, husbands over their wives and wives over their husbands.

The doings of God were then seen in His sanctuary. God's day was a delight and the congregation was alive in God's service. Everyone earnestly intent on the public worship. Every hearer eager to drink in the words of the minister as they came from his mouth. The assembly in general were from time to time in tears while the Word was preached. Some weeping with sorrow and distress, others with joy and love, others with pity and concern for the souls of their neighbors.

This is God visiting His people. Days of heaven on earth, the presidency of the Holy Spirit in the Church, life abundant given to God's people without measure.[4]

While reading this book, may you be ever mindful that revival comes only from above. Yet, in cooperation with all that God longs to do in our lives, may the flame of the next great awakening ignite each of our hearts and spread around the world.[5] As Samson once tied fiery foxtails together to scorch the work of the enemy, may we unite with God's Spirit to see the flames of revival spread, reaping the great harvest of souls God longs for.

The Breaker [the Messiah] will go up before them. They will break through, pass in through the gate and go out through it, and their King will pass on before them, the Lord at their head.[6]

Francis Anfuso
May 2012

---

4 Jones ML. What is Revival? Retrieved from ...Complete footnote: francisanfuso.com/awakened
5 1Corinthians 3:7, 2Corinthians 4:7
6 Micah 2:13 AMP

PROLOGUE: 40-YEAR ENIGMA

At the end of May 2012, having finished writing *AWAKENED*, God provided insight at a strategic moment that solved a four-decade quandary and gave further confirmation of the need for this book.

I've known for many years that my father was a friend of Israel. I remember once during my teen years meeting the Israeli Ambassador to the U.S. at a political dinner. But what has always been enigmatic to me is the picture below. It shows my father, Victor L. Anfuso, a five-term congressman, at the White House standing between President John F. Kennedy and Dr. David Ben-Gurion, the first Prime Minister of the modern state of Israel. I have spent many years musing over this picture. Did my father's special relationship with Israel have any spiritual significance for my own life?

History records that the original land God gave to the children of Israel had been lost due to their disobedience. Because of this rebellion, the Kingdoms of Israel and Judah were destroyed, and the remaining survivors taken as slaves by the armies of Assyria and Babylon. Eventually, these Jewish refugees were dispersed to many nations around the world. As the prophet Ezekiel predicted, their idolatry scattered them to "every wind" for nearly 2000 years.

Israel becoming a nation again is one of the greatest miracles of all time. After six million Jews were murdered during the Nazi holocaust of the early 1940s, the Jewish people were allowed to reoccupy much of the original land God had given them. On May 14, 1948, the Jewish People's Council declared the establishment of the State of Israel.

I remember as a teenager, after President Kennedy was assassinated, my dad asked my twin brother Joe and me if we were willing to move to Jerusalem. Since Lyndon Johnson had become president, my father was being considered for the U.S. Ambassadorship to Israel. Though my dad's health would soon fail, and this option would never materialize, for that moment the question was in play.

Another unusual connection with Israel was the fact that my first Holy Communion took place on May 14, 1955: the day of Israel's national anniversary. The picture below, taken from my First Communion Missal, puzzled me for many years.

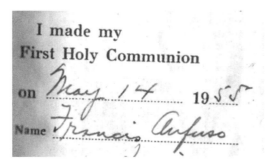

How ironic that I would receive my first Holy Communion on the 7th anniversary of this historic birthday of the nation of Israel.

The third mystifying event in connection to Israel and the date she became a nation was the fact that I was "born again" on May 14, 1972 — Israel's 24th anniversary as a new nation.

These three events had linked my life with the memorable May 14 date, and none of them were my doing:

1. My father's friendship with Dr. David Ben-Gurion and the restoration of Israel as a nation on May 14, 1948.

2. My first Holy Communion on May 14, 1955.

3. The day of my salvation, May 14, 1972.

The Bible says, "By the mouth of two or three witnesses every word shall be established."[7]

---

7 2Corinthians 13:1, NKJV

Year after year I did not understand why God allowed this sequence of events until a fourth connection with this date occurred on May 14, 2012. On that significant day, my 40th anniversary of following Jesus, I found myself in the nation of Wales filming the video connected with this book, retracing some of the people and places related to the historic Welsh Revival of 1904. This outpouring of God's Spirit is considered by many to be the greatest revival since the Day of Pentecost in the first century.

It seems apparent to me now, that for a reason known only to God, I needed to follow Jesus for a complete generation: 40 years. Eight days after this milestone, which I celebrated while in Wales, I was prompted by the Holy Spirit to read the book of Ezekiel. Upon doing so, I realized that Ezekiel's primary stewardships had been to challenge Israel about her sinful idolatry, to tell the nation that because of their rebellion they would be scattered to the four winds of the earth, but to leave them with a promise that a remnant would return to their ancestral land at some point in the future.[8]

Though my wife Suzie and I had visited the nation of Israel in 2004, and I have tried to cultivate a serious burden for the restoration of natural Israel, this vision never fully materialized. But as I reread the book of Ezekiel it finally jelled. Ezekiel was a prophet who ministered to the Jews during their captivity in Babylon. Though he spoke of their dissipation as a nation and their eventual scattering, he also prophesied the unthinkable, something that had never happened to any other dispersed people in the history of the world: the children of Israel would be re-gathered to their homeland. Ezekiel 37 rightly predicted that these dry bones would once again live.

I had mistakenly assumed the witness of these three May 14 events would in some way tie my relationship with *natural* Israel. But after reading the book of Ezekiel, the Lord showed me that my May 14 connection is to *spiritual* Israel, the Church—something I have always been passionate about.

8   Ezekiel 6:8; 11:17–19

In November 1972, I was ordained an Evangelist with a fiery commitment to Jesus, "to seek and save that which is lost."[9] Over the years, this burden has matured to help the Church return to occupy the land of her spiritual inheritance with God.

The following is a picture of me preaching in 1973 as a young, 24-year-old, newly saved evangelist.

I now see clearly that my father had a call to help *natural* Israel return to her promised land. My call is to see *spiritual* Israel, the Church, restored to her God-given inheritance, her rightful relationship with her loving Creator.[10] May the Church forsake her idolatry, repent of her sin, and experience a global outpouring of the Holy Spirit in order to be fully revived and the lost awakened.

This revelation not only provided an extraordinary understanding related to the four memorable May 14 dates, it further confirmed the burden to write this book. May you be challenged and even transformed as you read the marvelous things God has done throughout Church history, all of which is a foretaste of her glorious future.

Francis Anfuso
May 2012

---

9   Luke 19:10, NKJV

10   I understand the term, "Spiritual Israel" is not found in the Bible, but rather is implied in Romans 2:28–29 where Paul said by the Holy Spirit "For he is not a Jew who is one outwardly, nor is circumcision that which is outward in the flesh; but he is a Jew who is one inwardly; and circumcision is that of the heart, in the Spirit, not in the letter; whose praise is not from men but from God." I so look forward to the day when the walls of division are broken down and we become one flesh—with neither Jew nor Gentile; a day when we will all share in the wonderful promises of God and the inheritance of Abraham together according to Galatians 3:28–29 and Colossians 3:11.

FILMING IN WALES

(Written on the return flight home from Wales.)

The journey to the nation of Wales in May of 2012 with my wife, Suzie, and our videographer, Joel Sandvos, was both earth shaking and paradigm shifting. Suzie and I stayed in Island House, Evan Roberts' childhood home, and even slept in the room where Evan experienced nightly visitations with Jesus during a period of three months. We visited Blaenannerch Chapel and I prayed in the seat where Evan petitioned God, "Bend Me! Bend us!" 100,000 Welsh souls were converted in 1904, and then in the Moriah sanctuary where 1,200 packed in while hundreds more stood outside. It was awe-inspiring, challenging, intimidating, and unfathomable—events I will spend the rest of my life processing. Yet, while the experience exceeded our already-heightened expectations, it is what I didn't expect that seems most memorable, perplexing, and troubling.

The church in Wales is almost completely dormant. Only one-fourth of about 6,500 chapels were still operating in 2011, and more are closed down every week. The remaining houses of worship are attended by a handful of congregants; many are on a once-a-month rotation, only opened when a visiting pastor comes to lead the remnant of graying attendees. It is steeped in tradition with little passion, though the songs that are sung were surely written by grateful recipients of the abundant grace of God.

If I allowed myself, I could have easily been depressed. Instead, I comforted my soul and spirit with the eternal hope that these dry bones shall once again live. Yet, the most chilling by-product of our visit was the haunting reality that, barring a colossal outpouring of God's Spirit in America, we are hurling headlong to the same fate.

What happened to the nation of Wales? How could a once thriving church dissipate into a shell of its former flourishing self? There's only one explanation: at strategic moments when the eternal fate of a son or daughter, brother or sister, friend or neighbor, hung in the balance, someone gave up fighting for their soul. It's as simple and sad as that. I went to Wales gravely concerned. I left alarmed!

There is a significant difference between an alarmist and one sounding an alarm. An alarmist overreacts, exaggerates the danger, and causes needless worry or panic. Paul Revere wasn't an alarmist when he shouted, "The British are coming!" Nor was Jesus when He guaranteed, "Unless you repent you will all likewise perish."[11] I'm not an alarmist. I'm a realist.

More than ever I fully believe what God spoke to my heart a year ago: "Unless there is a mighty move of God in America, the Church cannot be revived, nor the lost awakened!" If I could see that the Church had a level of concern that in some way matched the urgency of her predicament, then I might take comfort in knowing she had accurately assessed the problem, and the solution would be forthcoming. Unfortunately, our present mindset is so inadequate our future is in grave peril. We are not making the necessary adjustments to meet the challenges we face.

I'm reminded of the King of Israel, Manasseh, who refused to humble himself before God and beg for mercy. A Babylonian army took him prisoner, "put a ring through his nose, bound him in bronze chains, and led him away to Babylon."[12] It appears this extreme level of wakeup call may be necessary before we are sufficiently aroused with an appropriate, desperate, intercessory burden.

As you read this book and watch the accompanying video, believe that what has been written and recorded understates the need of the hour. I only wish I was more spiritually awake myself to say it with the degree of clarity and passion it requires.

Even in the midst of the spiritual dryness that plagues much of the Western world, a renewed hunger nevertheless entreats the Lord to rain down an outpouring of His Spirit. It is my hope and prayer that this awakening occurring in some hearts will spread to many. It is of course God's desire for us. May we wholeheartedly respond!

Francis Anfuso
May 2012
francis@rockofroseville.com
francisanfuso.com

---

11 Luke 13:3
12 2Chronicles 33:10–11

CHAPTER 1:
DESPERATE
TIMES

"Is it the season of drought?
Is it the season of great heaviness and black clouds?
Then that is the season for showers."

—Charles Haddon Spurgeon

On April 18, 1906, a massive earthquake and subsequent fire left more than half of San Francisco's population homeless. It destroyed 28,000 buildings and killed as many as 3,000 people. Following the quake, fires broke out across the city from broken gas lines and stoves that had fallen over during the shaking. The fires spread quickly across San Francisco. Due to the quake's intensity most of the water mains in the city broke. To add to the confusion, San Francisco's fire chief became an early victim of falling debris. These factors compounded the magnitude of the destruction and desperation.

The next day, a serious aftershock rocked Los Angeles as well. It terrified residents who had just heard about the San Francisco earthquake and fire. Aware of their tenuous condition many were suddenly open to God.

A desperate circumstance had prepared the way for a mighty awakening.

Two months prior to the San Francisco quake, William J. Seymour arrived in Los Angeles. After praying one evening, the 34-year-old son of former slaves was baptized in the Holy Spirit and began holding public meetings. As the ground trembled, a glorious move of God erupted. By mid-May 1906, anywhere from 300 to 1,500 people attempted to fit into a building on a now-famous street called Azusa.[13,14] The Pentecostal Movement had been launched! At the writing of this book, it has over 600 million adherents worldwide.

A desperate time had become the backdrop for a glorious move of God.

It was hardly the first time.

GREAT SHAKINGS BEFORE GREAT AWAKENINGS

In his book, *The Spiritual Awakeners*, Keith Hardman says: "Revival is usually preceded by a time of spiritual depression, apathy, and gross sin, in which the great majority of nominal Christians are hardly different in any substantive way from members of secular society."[15] It is a well-documented historical fact that desperate needs within the culture and the church precede great outpourings of God's Spirit.

One of the men used as a driving force for a supernatural outpouring was a pastor from Northampton, Massachusetts, named Jonathan Edwards. Known to have authored the first detailed account of a revival, he is revered even today as a great evangelist.[16]

In the spring of 1734, two well-known young people met untimely deaths in Northampton. This tragedy had a remarkably sobering effect on the whole town. People began questioning the meaning of life, life after death, eternity, and other spiritual matters. Edwards seized the opportunity to answer questions and many were awakened to their need for Jesus. It was the spark that ignited the *First Great Awakening*.

---

13 Seymour J. Azusa Street Timeline. 2007 ...Complete footnote: francisanfuso.com/awakened

14 International Center for Spiritual Renewal...Complete footnote: francisanfuso.com/awakened

15 Hardman K. *The Spiritual Awakeners*. Chicago: Moody Press; 1983.

16 Edwards J. A Faithful Narrative of the Surprising ...Complete footnote: francisanfuso.com/awakened

At that time in New England, an alarming number of babies were born out of wedlock. When one of the most promiscuous women in Northampton was converted and began to reach out to her friends it further initiated a return to God.[17]

A few years prior, the condition of English society was also in dire need, "every sixth house became a gin shop. The poor were unspeakably wretched—over 160 crimes had the death penalty! Gin made the people what they were never before—cruel and inhuman. Hanging was a daily gala event. Those jerking on the ropes were watched and applauded by men, women and children who crowded the gallows for the best view. Prisons were unimaginable nightmares: young and old, hard crook and first offender were thrown together to fight for survival."[18]

Once again, a desperate state created a window for Heaven to come to Earth.

It would not last forever.

One of the unfortunate limitations found even in the most majestic moves of God is longevity. Though revival may see anguished souls come to God with an unforgettable fury, its duration is typically measured in months—certainly less than two years. And while it may well leapfrog around the globe for years, it has an end. All revivals have a finite shelf life. Perhaps this is due to our inability to retain the anointing of God in our fallen state. Like spiritual sponges, we become so saturated that we no longer remain focused and surrendered to God. Those who have attempted to prolong revival beyond God's actual presence inadvertently promote a spirit of imitation—a sad parody of the Spirit-filled original.

The principle here is: when in doubt...don't; when in faith... do!

---

17 Hansen C, Woodbridge J. *A God-Sized Vision: Revival Stories that Stretch and Stir.* Zondervan; 2010.

18 Pratney W. *Revival: Principles to Change the World.* Christian Life Books; 2002.

CHARACTERISTICS OF REVIVALS IN THE OLD TESTAMENT

Arthur Wallis described revival as "Divine intervention ...It is God revealing Himself to man in awesome holiness and irresistible power. It is man retiring into the background because God has taken the field. It is the Lord ...working in extraordinary power on saint and sinner."[19]

When studying revivals throughout history, the most instructive accounts come from the Bible itself. Dr. Wilbur Smith summarized nine principal characteristics of the eight major revivals in the Old Testament, each one relevant for us today.[20]

- Revivals occurred in a day of deep moral darkness and national depression.

- Revivals began in the heart of one consecrated servant of God who became the energizing power behind it, the agent used of God to quicken and lead the nation back to faith in God and to obedience in Him.

- Each revival rested on the Word of God and most were the result of preaching and proclaiming God's law with power.

- All revivals resulted in a return to the worship of Jehovah.

- All revivals witnessed the destruction of idols where they existed.

- All revivals recorded a subsequent separation from sin.

- All revivals promoted the return to blood sacrifices.

- Almost all recorded revivals show a restoration of great joy and gladness.

- Each revival was followed by a period of unusual national prosperity.[21]

19 Wallis A. *In the Day Of Thy Power.* CityHill Pub; 1990.
20 Pratney W. *Revival: Principles to Change the World.* Christian Life Books; 2002.
21 Fischer HA. *Reviving Revivals.* Gospel Publishing House; 1950.

Aren't we living in a day of great moral darkness and national depression? I venture to say that it's the greatest in my lifetime! So the question remains: are we willing to be those consecrated servants of God who return in faith and obedience to follow Jesus?

Will we proclaim God's Word and worship Him with all of our heart? Will we tear down our idols and allow the blood of Jesus Christ to separate and cleanse us from all of our sins? Only then will we experience a waterfall of joy and gladness washing over our obedient souls. Only then can God once again send the spiritual prosperity and blessing that comes from whole-heartedly following Jesus.

WHAT QUALIFIES AS DESPERATE?

If we define *desperate* as "a hopeless sense that a situation is so bad as to be impossible to deal with," can we then surmise that desperate times are presently hitting America and the Western world? Consider these facts taken from my book *Numb*, written in 2011.

- Sixty-five percent of the adult population in America is overweight, yet only 33 percent personally believe they are overweight.[22]

- Lifestyle changes can prevent over 50% of all cancers.[23]

- The U.S. is a world leader in youth homicide.[24]

- Self-violence among teens is the highest in recorded history. [25]

- More women than men are heads of households in the United States for the first time in American history.[26]

- The third leading cause of death for American teens is suicide.[27]

- Americans spend more money on slot machines

---

22 "Not too long ago in Western culture, obesity was... Complete footnote: francisanfuso.com/numb.
23 Danaei G, et al. Causes of cancer in the world... Complete footnote: francisanfuso.com/numb.
24 Teens are in great distress in our country. The U.S. is a... Complete footnote: francisanfuso.com/numb.
25 Self-violence in our teen population has increased... Complete footnote: francisanfuso.com/numb.
26 "Today, there are fewer boys who are successful... Complete footnote: francisanfuso.com/numb.
27 Suicide is the third most common cause of death for... Complete footnote: francisanfuso.com/numb.

(850,000 are in existence) than on movies, baseball, and theme parks combined.[28]

- Many people's entertainment habits exhibit symptoms comparable to a drug addict.[29]

- Sixty-four percent of Americans say they spend more time with their computer than with their significant other.[30]

- Fifty-six percent of divorce cases submitted to the American Academy of Matrimonial Lawyers involved "one party having an obsessive interest in pornographic websites," while 68% of divorce cases involve one spouse conducting an affair with someone they met over the Internet.[31]

- American teens are the most sexually active in history. Sixty percent of those 14 years and older in the United States have at least one sexually transmitted infection.[32]

- Daily pornographic search engine requests—68 million (25% of total search engine requests).[33]

- Most children in the U.S. will be exposed to hardcore pornography on the Internet by age 11; some say the average is as young as 8 years of age.[34]

- Teen pregnancy in the U.S. is 3 to 10 times higher than any other industrialized nation.[35]

- Teens who do not have sex before age 18 are nearly three times less likely to drop out of high school than teens who do have sex before age 18.[36]

- Seven of every ten teens who have been sexually active wish that they had waited until they were older.[37]

---

28 CBS News: 60 Minutes. Slot Machines: The Big Gamble... Complete footnote: francisanfuso.com/numb.

29 "Years of living vicariously through televised... Complete footnote: francisanfuso.com/numb.

30 According to a recent LiveScience survey, "64 percent... Complete footnote: francisanfuso.com/numb.

31 Fagan PF. The Quiet Family Killer: Pornography... Complete footnote: francisanfuso.com/numb.

32 Another example of self-injury is found in our country's... Complete footnote: francisanfuso.com/numb.

33 Every Man's Battle. Facts. 2011... Complete footnote: francisanfuso.com/numb.

34 In the US, the average age of first exposure to... Complete footnote: francisanfuso.com/numb.

35 University of North Carolina researchers demonstrated... Complete footnote: francisanfuso.com/numb.

36 "Beyond regrets of wishing they would have waited... Complete footnote: francisanfuso.com/numb.

37 Seven out of 10 teens that have been sexually active... Complete footnote: francisanfuso.com/numb.

- Nearly a third of university students (not just those who seek counseling) reported that in the last 12 months they've been so depressed that it's difficult to function.[38]

If these facts don't qualify as desperate, I don't know what would.

Even though our tolerance for the broken condition of the church and culture has become inflated or been dulled by medication and false comforts, it doesn't mean that our condition is any less precarious. Everyone learns the hard way. Some learn the really, really hard way. Sadly, some people never learn. It seems in this age that many people die, having never learned why they were alive.

GROSS DARKNESS COVERS THE EARTH

Conditions prior to historic revivals have always been desperate. The graver the times, the more primed for rejuvenation. In *The Spiritual Awakeners*, Keith Hardman writes: "Awakenings begin in periods of cultural distortion and grave personal stress, when we lose faith in the legitimacy of our norms, the viability of our institutions, and the authority of our leaders in church and state."[39]

John Wesley, one of the greatest revivalists of all time, arrived in New Castle, England in 1742 and wrote: "I was surprised; so much drunkenness, cursing (even from little children), do I never remember to have seen and heard before in so small a compass of time." He went on to say, "Surely this place is ripe for Him who came not to call the righteous, but sinners to repentance."[40]

History confirms—without exception—the depth of barrenness prior to a move of God. "From the year 1700 to the year of the French Revolution (1789), England seemed barren of all that is really good. Christianity seemed to lie as one dead. Morality, however much exalted in the pulpits, was thoroughly trampled underfoot in the streets. There was darkness in high places and

---

38 Gabriel T. Mental Health Needs Seen Growing at... Complete footnote: francisanfuso.com/numb.
39 Hardman K. *The Spiritual Awakeners*. Chicago: Moody Press; 1983.
40 Murray IH. *The Puritan Hope*. Carlisle, PA: Banner of Truth; 1971.

darkness in low places… darkness in the country, and darkness in the town…a gross, thick religious and moral darkness—a darkness that might be felt."[41]

The great Christian historian J. Edwin Orr wrote, "Prior to the Second Great Awakening of the early 19th century when the colonial population totaled 5,000,000, 300,000 were drunkards, 15,000 died annually."[42] And "The major U.S. colleges (Harvard, Princeton, Williams, Dartmouth) were almost totally non-Christian, Christians on campuses were so few and so unpopular that they met in secret like a communist cell and kept their minutes in code to avoid mistreatment. Students burned buildings, forced presidents to resign, destroyed Bibles and profaned public worship."[43]

As society withers, initially churches suffer. It takes a while for shell-shocked believers to find their spiritual sea legs during cultural storms. But, eventually, they do. A cry goes forth from the camp that awakens the sleeping giant. As revival author Sean Smith states it is not a coincidence that "the declining Church becomes the desperate Church."[44]

Societal conditions were not as critical in 1830 as they were in 1727 and 1792 prior to the First and Second Great Awakenings. Consequently, the revival did not impact the culture to the same degree. How ironic that what we chafe at is invariably for our own good. The lesson? Do not lament challenges that bring you to your knees. Instead, with humility, rejoice before the God who sends help in your great time of need.

EXTREME MEASURES

If your child was ill and their future in peril, if it was a sickness that would eventually take their life, would you do whatever it takes to save them? Would you pay whatever price necessary to see them healed, even if it meant incredible sacrifice? If it changed

41   Ryle JC. *Christian Leaders of the 18th Century.* Carlisle, PA: Banner of Truth; 1978.

42   Orr JE. The Re-Study of Revival and Revivalism, 1981.

43   Orr JE. The Re-Study of Revival and Revivalism, 1981.

44   Smith S. *I Am Your Sign.* Destiny Image, Inc.; 2011.

how you lived—would you do it? If it cost you everything—would you still be "all in"?

In the physical realm, many people would do whatever it takes to save someone they love. A father would protect. A mother would nurture. A brother, sister, or friend would lay down their lives. But in the spirit realm, it's so much more difficult to connect the dots.

Why is the eternal struggle between Heaven and Hell less real than the temporary battles on Earth? Compared to eternity, Earth is a moment. Why do we spend so much time obsessing over our one-night motel, and so little energy cultivating a relationship with the Creator of our eternal home? Why would we give our own blood in order to physically save those we love, and yet not fully believe Christ's blood alone is able to save those He loves?

If others said it was impossible, would we give up, conceding, "There's nothing I can do?" If enemies tried to persuade us it was hopeless, would we believe them? If we knew the eternal destiny of those we loved was in some tangible way in our court, that we were a difference maker as to where they would spend eternity, would that sufficiently motivate us to step up—to awaken to our true responsibility?

REVIVAL: GOD'S WORK, NOT MAN'S

Revival is the outpouring of the Holy Spirit. It is not the work of man. It is the work of God. Duncan Campbell, the man God used in the great *Hebridean Revival* of 1949 said, "In revival, the community suddenly becomes conscious of the presence of God in a matter of hours—not days. Something is happening that draws men and women to the house of God. You find within hours, scores of men and women crying to God for mercy.[45]

During the nine years after my conversion, I was unclear about how to hear the distinct, inner voice of God. One day the Spirit of God gave me an impression that He was going to teach me to hear His voice so that I could teach others. Over the next few years, I spent much time praying and fasting, dissecting the Four Gospels and Book of Acts. It resulted in a textbook and seminar entitled *Spirit-Led Evangelism*. For 15 years

---

45 Campbell D. *The Revival Study Bible.*

following, I ministered in the gifts of the Spirit over thousands of people. I still regularly receive communications from those whose lives were transformed during that season.

When I first began to move in God's spiritual gifts amongst congregations with high anticipation, I was aware of the pressure to operate in my own strength.[46] Consequently, I would make a focused commitment to *do nothing*, until God chose to *do something*. Though He consistently did, it required great patience and a refusal to please the crowd, which would have grieved the Holy Spirit and been, at best, manipulation.

Scripture confirms, "Unless the LORD builds the house, those who build it labor in *vain*.Unless the LORD watches over the city, the watchman stays awake in vain."[47] No matter how desperate we are to see God move, no matter how agonizing it is to watch the church flounder and the culture plunge into deception, we must never allow fear, frustration or man pleasing to draw us away from being led by the Holy Spirit.

Revival comes from God alone!

---

46 1Corinthians 12:1–11

47 Psalm 127:1, ESV

PRAYER DURING DESPERATE TIMES

"God does not answer prayer, He answers desperate prayer."[48]

"Lord Jesus, You faced difficulties that I cannot even imagine when You became sin for me, when You were separated by that sin from Your Father in Heaven, and when you died an excruciating death on the Cross. As You had joy while withstanding those difficulties, give me the joyful assurance I need to stand in all seasons. Give me complete faith that you will always protect my fragile life.

"So, Lord, 'I cry to You for help when my heart is overwhelmed. Lead me to the towering rock of safety...'[49] I know that because You hold my heart in the palm of Your hand, You desire me to overcome and not be overwhelmed. Please keep me from stumbling, for You alone watch over my soul. You have promised not to slumber or sleep, to keep me safe during the storms of life."[50]

QUESTIONS FOR GROUP DISCUSSION

1. What desperate present condition of the culture disturbs you the most? Consider the following areas: economic, moral, spiritual, or other.

2. Is there a desperate dimension you presently struggle with the most? Why?

3. How would you describe your faith level to believe that God is using the present desperate dimensions for your good and His glory?

4. How do you believe God is using desperate dimensions within the culture and church to fulfill His will?

5. What "shaking" have you experienced recently? How has it made you desperate to change personally?

---

48 Reid A. ROAR: The Deafening Thunder of Spiritual...Complete footnote: francisanfuso.com/awakened
49 Psalm 61:2, NLT
50 Psalm 121:3

CHAPTER 2:
LIFE AND DEATH PRAYERS

"God has sent you into this dark valley for nothing less than to raise these doom-struck creatures from the dead. That is your mission..."

—General William Booth, Founder of the Salvation Army

What will it take for lost souls to be drawn, convicted, and converted?

During revival, Heaven and Hell break loose as the God of whirlwinds swirls! Whatever is not secure in Him is soon swept away. A perfect storm descends upon the unjust and just, the evil and the good.[51] If we walk in light then God brightens our path, if we cling to darkness it consumes us. We miss our best hope.

God's tempest is not meant to satisfy us but rather to solidify our foundation in Him. If we are joined to Jesus our lives are safe. Whether left hooks arrive from Heaven or Hell makes little difference. For as our paths mesh in the stability of God's plan, every test works for our good and His glory.[52]

---

51 Matthew 5:44–46a
52 Romans 8:28

When Jesus said of Himself that "the ruler of this world is coming. He has no claim on me," He knew His very life was embedded in His Father alone.[53] So must ours be! For the path of life is only found in Him! Leonard Ravenhill said it this way, "Jesus did not come into the world to make bad men good. He came into the world to make dead men live!"

DEAD MEN LIVING

I was once dead but am now alive in Jesus.

It was prayer that made the difference.

My mother was an intercessor. She fervently prayed for all five of her wayward children. She prayed while we dodged near death experiences. During the later years of her life, she interceded not just for us but also for hundreds of others by name. Now, 40 years later, we still live whole-heartedly for Jesus.

In 1973, my twin brother Joseph was living in India and Nepal in order to fully immerse himself in Eastern religions. While he was overseas, our two sisters and one brother had given their hearts to Jesus. We were all particularly concerned for Joseph, not having heard any word from him in over six months. My sister Maria's husband, George, who had experienced a dramatic conversion, felt so unsettled about Joseph's wellbeing that he committed to a seven day fast.

We didn't realize the impact of these seven days of prayer and fasting until some time later. Their effect was nothing short of miraculous. During the exact days George was interceding for Joseph, Joseph was in Delhi, India. While in his room meditating, a cross of light illuminated the door and God spoke to his spirit with these words, "Jesus is the way."[54]

It was divine intervention!

Because Joseph was experiencing a number of meta-physical phenomena, this event did not cause him to surrender to Jesus.

---

53 John 14:30, ESV
54 John 14:6

But it certainly served as a catalyst to point him in the direction of his sisters' and brother's newfound faith in Jesus Christ.

Within a few weeks, Joseph returned to the United States. A short time later, surrendered his life to Jesus. Since 1983, he has directed Forward Edge, a Christian relief and mission's organization that sends hundreds of teams around the world to share Christ's love with those affected by poverty, disaster, and sickness. Our family knows firsthand the power of prayer.

BEING ACCURSED FOR OTHERS

One of the most remarkable demonstrations of a life and death prayer is recorded by a great figure in the New Testament, Paul the Apostle. He was so burdened for his lost countrymen, the Jewish nation, that he wrote, "I am speaking the truth in Christ—I am not lying; my conscience bears me witness in the Holy Spirit—that I have great sorrow and unceasing anguish in my heart."[55]

What would cause his heart to break so profoundly? Could it be a need in his personal life? Hardly! Paul writes, "For I could wish that I myself were accursed and cut off from Christ for the sake of my brothers, my kinsmen according to the flesh."[56] The scope of this wish is almost unfathomable. The word cursed used here is the Greek word *anathema*, which means "condemned to Hell."

Paul, filled with sorrow and anguish for his lost countrymen, wished that he be sentenced to Hell in their stead. If that is not a life and death prayer, I don't know what is. To die for someone demonstrates an extraordinary act of love, but what depth of love does a person lay bare who is willing to go to Hell for another?

Who would do that?

Actually many believe this is exactly what Jesus did for us when He became the embodiment of sin. He suffered and died, then went to Hell in our place.[57] Such depth of love cannot be fully fathomed.

---

55 Roman 9:1–2, ESV
56 Roman 9:3, ESV
57 1Peter 3:18–19

Moses likewise expressed another astonishing life and death prayer when he came down from a mountaintop experience with God only to find the nation of Israel rebelling. Moses' intercessory prayer was remarkable: "Alas, this people have sinned a great sin. They have made for themselves gods of gold. But now, if You will forgive their sin—but if not, please blot me out of Your book that You have written."[58] Once again a fully surrendered intercessor was willing to relinquish his life in order to spare others.

Have you ever considered the possibility that the most strategic person to pray and believe for the salvation of those you love is... you? You may be their best shot at dodging Hell and entering Heaven. If this is so, perhaps the real need is that you wake up and begin to pray life and death prayers on their behalf. A glorious eternal destiny may depend upon it.

I know my mother's prayers were life and death for me.

THIS KIND COMES OUT...

Are we separated from God's supernatural hand by various sins that limit His ability to move on our behalf? Do fear, unbelief, doubt, and other impurities contaminate the flow of God's anointed power through us? "The Lord's arm is not too weak to save you, nor is His ear too deaf to hear you call. It's your sins that have cut you off from God. Because of your sins, He has turned away and will not listen anymore."[59]

In the Old Testament, Nehemiah describes the pitiful condition of his beloved city Jerusalem. "The survivors who are left from the captivity in the province are there in great distress and reproach. The wall of Jerusalem is also broken down, and its gates are burned with fire."[60] Because of genuine concern he "sat down and wept, and mourned for many days…fasting and praying before the God of heaven."[61]

---

58   Exodus 32: 31–32, ESV
59   Isaiah 59:1–2
60   Nehemiah 1:3
61   Nehemiah 1:4

Rather than complain about the precarious situation before him, he took personal responsibility for the sins and poor judgments of his ancestors. His outcry perfectly corresponds to the pressing need of this critical hour: "God help us! Bring us together in prayer and fasting, so that we may entreat you to move Heaven and Earth."

In the years to come, God is going to use fasting and prayer as a weapon in the battle for the hearts and minds of men. The Supernatural Church will arise as it humbles itself. A new generation of whole-hearted disciples will seek to overcome evil with good by yielding to God's divine disciplines. Paul wrote, "I have worked hard and long, enduring many sleepless nights. I have been hungry and thirsty and have often gone without food."[62]

All men deserve our prayers and tears.

Before Paul's conversion, he was Saul of Tarsus, the archenemy of the fledgling Christian faith. Even while condemning Christ-followers to death, hot tears were being prayed for him. Because of this, Paul would later write, "Brothers, my heart's desire and prayer to God for them is that they may be saved."[63] When our heart's desire is at last joined to God's deepest longing, a magnificent melting takes place. That which was once frozen becomes fluid in the hands of a merciful Creator.

In his book, *Why Revival Tarries*, Leonard Ravenhill states that "the reason revival doesn't come is because there is no revival cry. God seems to wait until there is a cry for revival coming from a core of people. There must be prayer for the outpouring in order for the outpouring to come."[64]

WINNING THE AIR WAR

With the advent of modern warfare, a strategy has immerged that decisively renders the enemy powerless. It is air combat. An assault from above effectively wins the Spirit battle just as it conquers literal ground wars.

---

62   2Corinthians 11:27a

63   Romans 10:1

64   Ravenhill L. *Why Revival Tarries*. Bethany House Publishers; 1959.

Some have been naïve to the power of the air. Just prior to the First World War, one general quipped: "Aviation is fine as a sport. But as an instrument of war, it is worthless."[65] In 1937, another military leader lacked similar insight. "It is not possible... to concentrate enough military planes with military loads over a modern city to destroy that city."[66]

President Franklin D. Roosevelt was more astute in his observation of the full potential of air power when he remarked, "Hitler built a fortress around Europe, but he forgot to put a roof on it."

Several years prior to World War II, British Prime Minister Stanley Baldwin told his governmental leaders, "I think it is well...for the man in the street to realize there is no power on earth that can protect him from bombing, whatever people may tell him. The bomber will always get through."[67] Three years later, upon learning that Germany had secretly built an air force in defiance of the Treaty of Versailles, Baldwin lamented, "I wish for many reasons flying had never been invented."[68]

Air power—like fire power—is a neutral zone that can avail for either good or evil. When it comes to prayer, a comparable counterpart to the expression, "Fight fire with fire!" would be, "Only air power can defeat air power."[69]

At the end of the day, whoever wins the hearts and minds of men wins their souls, and that is always a life and death issue. That's why, "Air power is like poker. A second-best hand is like none at all."[70]

Even Benjamin Franklin futuristically mused, "And where is the Prince who can afford to so cover his country with troops for its defense, as that ten thousand men descending from the clouds, might not in many places do an infinite deal of mischief, before a force could be brought together to repel them?"

---

65 General Ferdinand Foch, Professor of Strategy, Ecole Superiure de Guere, 1911.

66 U.S. Colonel John W. Thomason Jr., November 1937.

67 Stanley Baldwin, British Prime Minister, House of Commons speech, 10 November 1932.

68 British Prime Minister Stanley Baldwin, 1935.

69 Major Alexander P. de Seversky, United States Army Air Forces.

70 General George Kenney, Commander of Allied Air Forces in the Southwest Pacific, 1942–1945.

God is not watching reruns in Heaven. He makes all things new, even certain aspects of spiritual warfare.[71] As each Heaven-birthed revival is in some significant way unique, so too successful assaults from Hell are varied and unpredictable. The natural parallel mimics the supernatural. "The military mind always imagines that the next war will be on the same lines as the last."[72]

A concentrated season of prayer and fasting relentlessly bombards from above.

When you feel overwhelmed by the enemy—PRAY! Call upon God and His armies in Heaven to assault Earth from above. As it works in the natural, it will work in the Spirit. God will repel the enemy's assault.

A Japanese infantry commander noted this principle during the Second World War, "We have the enemy surrounded. We are dug in and have overwhelming numbers. But enemy airpower is mauling us badly. We will have to withdraw."[73]

Prayer is decisive. "Air warfare is a shot through the brain, not a hacking-to-pieces of the enemy's body."[74] "The only proper defense is offense."[75] PRAY!

Defensive responses, without a plan of attack, guarantee defeat. The gates of Hell can't fly. We must strike offensively in prayer and intercession. "It is not possible to seal an air space hermetically by defensive tactics."[76]

The Bible speaks clearly of the aerial nature of our warfare: "the prince of the power of the air, the spirit that is now at work in the sons of disobedience" will be defeated. God's Word promises, "they have conquered him by the blood of the Lamb and by the word of their testimony, for they loved not their lives even unto death."[77]

---

71 Revelation 21:5

72 Marshal of France Ferdinand Foch.

73 A Japanese infantry commander, situation report to headquarters, Burma, WW II.

74 Major General J.F.C. Fuller, British Army.

75 Air Vice-Marshal J.E. "Johnnie" Johnson, Royal Air Force.

76 ibid

77 Revelation 12:11, ESV

Prayer is not just the ultimate weapon. It is the ultimate advantage. "There is something more important than any ultimate weapon. That is the ultimate position—the position of total control over Earth…Whoever gains that ultimate position gains control, total control, over the Earth, for the purposes of tyranny or for the service of freedom."[78]

Jesus told us that all of the power and authority in Heaven and Earth has now been given to us.[79] There is nothing more powerful touching the throne of God than the prayers of His saints. "The weapons we fight with are not the weapons of the world. On the contrary, they have divine power to demolish strongholds."[80] God's divine power is waiting to be released.

PRAYER AND FASTING THROUGHOUT HISTORY

Jesus said, "Blessed are those who hunger and thirst for righteousness, for they shall be filled."[81] Since the beginning of time food has been the center of many spiritual battles.

Adam and Eve plunged the entire human race into sin over an issue involving food.[82] Esau sold his birthright for a hot meal.[83] The Israelites murmured against God in the wilderness because of food and consequently lost His blessing.[84] And the infamous city Sodom was guilty of the sin of "fullness of food."[85]

As food is important to us, so it is to God. He created food to nourish both our body and soul, and it certainly does. I love food. I'm Italian and grew up spending serious time eating. Though food is vital, it's no substitute for our relationship with God. There are times when, in order to demonstrate our commitment to the fulfillment of God's will, we must learn to fast and pray. Jesus said, "My food is to do the will of Him who sent Me, and to finish His work."[86]

---

78   Senator Lyndon B. Johnson, 1958.

79   Matthew 28:18

80   2Corinthians 10:4, NIV

81   Matthew 5:6, NKJV

82   Genesis 3:6

83   Genesis 25:34

84   Numbers 11:4,5; 21:5; Psalm 78:29–31

85   Ezekiel 16:49

86   John 4:34, NKJV

Esther, a godly queen, abstained from food and water along with her countrymen to beseech God for salvation from certain destruction.[87] Each of us will know God's provision as we fast and pray.

Anna, an 84-year old Jewish widow served God with fasting and prayer, night and day.[88] Anna's faithfulness to this commitment enabled her to witness baby Jesus' first visit to the temple. We too will see Jesus more clearly as we fast and pray.

Acts chapter 27 records Paul and a Roman ship's crew fasting for fourteen days. This act of belief, combined with Paul's obedience to God's directions, resulted in the rescue of all 276 members from certain death. Each of us will experience the supernatural power of Jesus as we fast and pray.

The worldwide missionary movement began in the early Church as members ministered to the Lord and fasted.[89] Great spiritual movements and revivals owe their birth to prayer and fasting.

According to the Bible, a disciple should fast in order to:

- *Act in obedience to God's Word.*[90] Jesus prophesied, "the day will come when the bridegroom will be taken away from them, and then they will fast."[91]

- *Receive the grace and power of God.*[92] King David said, "I humble myself with fasting."[93]

- Overcome temptations.[94] When Jesus was tempted in the wilderness, He fasted.[95]

- *Be purified from sin* (either from our sins or the sins of others).[96] When the people of Nineveh believed God, they proclaimed a fast and put on sackcloth, from the greatest to the least of them.[97]

---

87   Esther 4:16
88   Luke 2:37
89   Acts 13
90   Isaiah 58:6–9; Joel 2:12; 2Corinthians 6:4–5; 11:27; Matthew 17:21
91   Matthew 9:15
92   James 4:10; Philippians 2:8; Psalm 35:13; 69:10; 1Peter 5:5,6; Deuteronomy 9:3–4; Ezra 8:21; 2Chronicles 7:14
93   Psalm 35:13
94   Matthew 9:15–17
95   Luke 4:1–2,14
96   Daniel 9:3; 1Samuel 7:6; Nehemiah 9:1–2; Jonah 3:5
97   Jonah 3:5

- *Become weak so God's power can be strong.*[98] The Psalmist wrote, "My knees are weak through fasting..."[99]

- *Obtain God's support in order to accomplish His will.*[100] The Church at Antioch fasted and prayed when they sent Barnabas and Saul.[101]

- *Ask for God's help in a difficult situation.*[102] King David fasted and pleaded with God for the life of his child.[103]

- *Seek God's direction.*[104] The great prophet Daniel fasted and prayed and heard from God.[105]

- *Provide understanding when studying the Bible or seeking divine revelation.*[106] Hannah prayed and fasted and God answered her prayers.[107]

Much of this book was written during a 40-day fast; my stomach was empty, but my heart was full of inspiration from above. As we prepare our hearts to pray, fast, and seek God, may we keep our eyes on the true prize—knowing Jesus. "You have said, 'Seek my face.' My heart says to you, 'Your face, LORD, do I seek.'"[108]

REVIVALISTS AND PRAYER

The modern 24-7 prayer movement has a number of ancient pedigrees. On August 10, 1727, residents on Count Nicolas Zinzendorf's German Estates began an uninterrupted prayer meeting, which lasted 100 years. In modern times, the International House of Prayer (IHOP), Kansas City, has established continual prayer since September 1999. They have significantly influenced my own life and prayer around the world.

---

98 2Corinthians 12:9–10
99 Psalm 109:24
100 Acts 14:23
101 Acts 13:3
102 Esther 4:16; Matthew 17:21; Isaiah 58:6
103 2Samuel 12:16
104 Ezra 8:21,23
105 Daniel 10
106 Jeremiah 36:6; Daniel 1:8–17; 10:7; Acts 10:10
107 1Samuel 1:17
108 Psalm 27:8, ESV

Whether prayer is *continuous* or not, it must be *consistent.* The great revivalist and evangelist Charles Finney knew that prayer was the indispensable condition to promote revival. He said: "Unless I had the experience of prayer I could do nothing. If even for a day or an hour I lost the spirit of grace and supplication. I found myself unable to preach with power and efficiency, or to win souls by personal conversation."[109] When Finney did not see the desired results in a revival he prayed and fasted, often praying four hours a day. "He marked his work with great prayer feeling that unless he could pray through, no revival would be possible."[110]

In 1857, an awakening of businessmen and women became known as "The Prayer Meeting Revival." A layman, Jeremiah Lanphier, started daily prayer meetings that, within three months, had multiplied to over 100 prayer gatherings of 50,000 people throughout New York City. Over a period of 18 months, one million people were converted throughout the U.S. A comparable revival today could result in the salvation of 10 million people.

Perhaps no revival had a greater impact than the Welsh Revival. "Begun with prayer meetings of less than a score of intercessors [a score is 20], when it burst its bounds the Churches of Wales were crowded for more than two years."[111] Prayer and praise characterized this phenomenal move of God.

Evan Roberts prayed 13 months for a wave of revival to come. David Matthews, who was present at the 1904 Welsh Revival, said of Evan Roberts: "Prayer was the keynote of his tireless life. No action taken or entered into was done so without definitely committing the matter to God. His soul appeared to be saturated through with the spirit of prayer. It was the atmosphere in which he moved and lived...whenever one looked on his face, he seemed engaged in intercession."[112]

---

109 Miller B. *Charles Finney.* Bethany House Publishers; 1969.
110 ibid.
111 Orr JE. The Re-Study of Revival and Revivalism, 1981.
112 Matthews D. *I Saw the Welsh Revival.* Christian Life Books; 2002.

In preparation for God to move, prior to the significant outpouring in April of 1906 and the move to Azusa Street, William Seymour prayed five to seven hours a day. When the revival finally broke out, they held services three times a day, seven days a week, for three years. At times, 800 people filled the inside of the primitive building, formerly a stable for horses, while another 500 worshipped and prayed outside in the dirt.

It's been said, "Revival turns careless living into vital concern... exchanges self-indulgence for self-denial. Yet, revival is not a miraculous visitation, falling on an unprepared people like a bolt out of the blue. It comes when God's people earnestly want revival and are willing to pay the price."[113]

The Lord offers every generation this glorious promise. For those who are willing, He assures: "If My people who are called by My name will humble themselves, and pray and seek My face, and turn from their wicked ways, then I will hear from heaven, and will forgive their sin and heal their land." [114]

113 Miller B. *Charles Finney*. Bethany House Publishers; 1969.
114 ibid

LIFE AND DEATH PRAYER

"Jesus, I know there are crucial needs all around me that truly are life and death. Though, as one person, I can attempt to meet only a few of these needs. Please direct my prayers to those individuals whom I can help, and give me the wisdom to know how to pray for them, love them, and serve them. I trust that You will lead and guide me by Your Spirit.

"Lord, I also pray for my unsaved loved ones, particularly those who are not ready to face You in eternity. Convict their hearts of their need for You. Use whatever means necessary to get their attention. Awaken them out of the fog of their unbelief, the deception of their rebellion, and the folly of their stubbornness. In Jesus name, I pray!"

QUESTIONS FOR GROUP DISCUSSION

1. Do you believe your own salvation was in part due to someone's specific prayers? Who?

2. In what other ways have life and death prayers impacted your life? Your family?

3. Have you fasted before? What motivated you to start a fast?

4. Do you believe that God has commissioned you to specifically pray for someone in particular? If so, who?

5. What adjustments do you need to make in your life to take intercessory life and death prayers seriously for those He has placed upon your heart?

CHAPTER 3: GIFT OF REPENTANCE

"I consider the chief dangers that confront the coming century will be religion without the Holy Ghost, Christianity without Christ, forgiveness without repentance, politics without God, and heaven without hell."

—General William Booth, Founder of the Salvation Army

I was dramatically saved in a revival—a sovereign, rescuing act of God broke the chains of deception over my life. With tears, I knelt and surrendered to Jesus. Streams of living water flowed into my heart, and I've never been the same since.[115] It was 1972, and hundreds of seekers journeyed to a community of "Jesus Freaks" in Smartsville, a little northern California gold rush town of just 200 people. At the end of our Sunday worship services a hundred of us would pile in the back of pickup trucks. We would drive five miles to the Yuba River in Timbuctoo, baptizing as many as 15 people each week.

But not everyone was excited about what God was doing.

When longhaired, barefoot hippies lined the front of the church to receive Jesus, a few of the old folks who had prayed for revival were offended and left the church. They had thought they wanted what God wanted, but—in the end—they exited disappointed. Sadly, this is a common dilemma in revival.

---

115 John 7:38
116 The Gospel Truths. Quotes of Leonard Ravenhill. ...Complete footnote: francisanfuso.com/awakened

Church as usual doesn't scare the devil. That's when he feels most safe. It's when leaders and congregants break and allow God to have His way that all Heaven breaks lose. Leonard Ravenhill says it like this, "If there's no brokenness in the pulpit, why should there be any brokenness in the pew?"[116]

We tend to think God's clear exhortation in scripture doesn't fully apply to us. "'For My thoughts are not your thoughts, neither are your ways My ways,' declares the LORD. 'For as the heavens are higher than the earth, so are My ways higher than your ways and My thoughts than your thoughts.'"[117]

God's declarations transcend all generations.

This verse alone should trigger a massive heads-up that God's move among us will always look different than we expect. Likewise, our response will dictate whether we see prayer answered or experience a sinking sense that we missed God. To avoid that disappointment, God charges us. "He has shown you, O man, what is good; and what does the LORD require of you but to do justly, and to love mercy, and to walk humbly with your God?"[118] A humble heart before God ensures we have a part in what God desires to do.

STRATEGY OF HUMILITY

When it comes to sin, we can wait to get caught, or we can turn ourselves in.

The former resists connection to God. The latter opens up an intimate relationship with our Creator that unlocks the essence of our existence. If, as the Bible states, "God opposes the proud, but gives grace to the humble," then humility is the key to our success in seeing God move.[119,120] In a full-blown revival, people rush to get right with God, and therefore are eager to humble themselves before Him, even doing things they would have considered humiliating.

---

117 Isaiah 55:8–9, ESV
118 Micah 6:8, NKJV
119 James 4:6, ESV
120 1Peter 5:6
121 Smith S. *I Am Your Sign*. Destiny Image, Inc.; 2011.

This heart-felt humility not only impacts the church, but the culture as well. "Deep down inside, the world wants to see someone who believes in something strong enough that they'll sacrifice. The ability to lovingly push all our chips in the middle of the table will gain not only their attention, but also their hearts."[121]

What will it take to see other people's hearts spiritually transformed? Exactly what it would take for ours as well— a willingness to fully surrender, take responsibility for our actions, and repent of our sins.

> *Repentance is a radical act, but it's more than the initial confession. It must become an ongoing lifestyle. The inner history of revivals is characterized by a strong sense of dissatisfaction. The pleasures of the world fail to bring any satisfaction. People wake up to a realization that trading heavenly joys for earthly joys is a sorry trade-off with serious loss. Revival has always begun because of repentance manifested through radical obedience.*[122]

In order for this to happen, God's heart must become our heart. Only then will the Holy Spirit pour out His saving grace. "For godly grief produces a repentance that leads to salvation without regret, whereas worldly grief produces death."[123]

What precedes a revival? "An individual or small group of God's people becomes conscious of its sins and backslidden condition and vows to forsake all that is displeasing to God."[124] Ian Malins, author of *Prepare the Way for Revival*, says, "There can be no revival without a fresh awareness of the holiness of God, the depth of sin, and a deep and lasting turning back to God in repentance."[125]

Before the Welsh Revival of 1904 began, a minister named Seth Joshua while closing a difficult meeting in prayer, entreated the Lord, "Bend us!" Evan Roberts heard his broken cry. It was the spark he needed. Over and over again Evan pleaded with the Lord, "Bend me! Bend us!" A month later, a spiritual brush fire began that would sweep across Wales and around the world.

---

122 Smith S. *I Am Your Sign*. Destiny Image, Inc.; 2011.

123 2Corinthians 7:10, ESV

124 Hardman K. *The Spiritual Awakeners*. Chicago, IL: Moody Press; 1983.

125 Malins I. *Prepare the Way for Revival*. Grand Rapids, MI: Chosen Books; 2004.

"For thus says the High and Lofty One Who inhabits eternity, whose name is Holy: 'I dwell in the high and holy place, with him who has a contrite and humble spirit, to revive the spirit of the humble, and to revive the heart of the contrite ones.'"[126] Contrite here literally means to "grind down, to wear away." Revival comes to those who have allowed self-centeredness to be ground down and worn away.[127] Our ability to repent is a gift. It cannot be earned or deserved. But it can be asked for, longed for and received.

Humility is the first step on the road to revelation.

The second is repentance.

HISTORY OF REPENTANCE IN REVIVALS

Revival and repentance have always been joined. It's been rightly said, "Revival is agonizing: It so terrorizes you over your sin that you repent deeply. Revival is consuming: It leaves you no time for hobbies, for chores around the house, for work, or sleep. Revival wrecks your appointment calendar, interrupts TV times, demands your full attention...and wears you out."[128]

And we wonder why revivals are so rare.

Charles Finney, the premiere revivalist of the 1800s, said, "We can expect a revival when the sinfulness of sinners grieves and distresses Christians."[129]

Frank Bartleman, the intercessor and journalist used by God in the Azusa Street Revival concurred saying, "The depth of your repentance will determine the height of your revival."[130]

The word repent in the Bible is the Greek word *metanoia*. It means "to change your mind; reconsider; or, to think differently."[131] The apostle Peter admonished the first century followers of Jesus,

---

126 Isaiah 57:15
127 Smith S. *I Am Your Sign.* Destiny Image, Inc.; 2011.
128 Towns EL, Porter D, Towns E. The Ten Greatest Revivals Ever. Vine Books; 2000.
129 Smith S. I Am Your Sign. Destiny Image, Inc.; 2011.
130 ibid.
131 Strong's Exhaustive Bible Concordance, from 3326 and 3539.
132 Acts 3:19, ESV

"Repent therefore, and turn again, that your sins may be blotted out, that times of refreshing may come from the presence of the Lord..."[132]

Turn away! Change your mind! Think differently! Repent!

If repentance is mandatory for a move of God, how does one repent? Unfortunately, this is a forgotten practice in many feel-good churches in America.

One important key to repenting rightly is remembering I can be no more holy in public than I am in private. Likewise there are times when I must confess my private sin to others. "Confess your sins to one another and pray for one another, that you may be healed. The prayer of a righteous person has great power as it is working."[133]

Sean Smith writes, "The world doesn't cry out until the followers of Christ first cry out, come clean, and throw themselves into the currents of God's dealings. Emerging revivalists are given a holy understanding of their times and the urgency of the hour. J. Edwin Orr said this: 'The Church will be moved when its members are moved.'"[134,135]

What are the effects of genuine repentance upon the church and the culture? Though the primary theme of the Welsh revival was "love," its fruit was repentance. "The churches of Wales were crowded for more than two years; 100,000 outsiders were converted, drunkenness was cut in half, taverns went bankrupt. Crime was so diminished that judges were presented with white gloves signifying there were no cases of murder, assault, rape, robbery or the like to consider. The police became 'unemployed' in many districts."[136] Another account states, "Coalmines stopped work with transport difficulties. The pit ponies didn't understand their instruction; they couldn't recognize their owner's 'cleaned-up' language! At least 75% of the converts were still true after five years."[137]

For centuries, the nation of Wales has been an unusual recipient of grace for revival. Perhaps that's why "Welsh theologians have

133 James 5:16, ESV
134 Smith S. *I Am Your Sign*. Destiny Image, Inc.; 2011.
135 Orr J.E. The Church Must First Repent, 1937.
136 Towns EL, Porter D, Towns E. The Ten Greatest Revivals Ever. Vine Books; 2000.
137 Pratney W. *Revival: Principles to Change the World*. Createspace; 2010.

said that the three great characteristics of classic revival are:

1. Heartfelt desire to be free from all sin and any impurities of heart;
2. Powerful impact on the wider community; and
3. Intense, palpable, and extraordinary sense of God's presence"[138]

Helen Rosevear, a veteran missionary who was interviewed about the Belgian Congo Revival in the 1950s, reported a comparable experience of transformation. She shared these insights:

What was the strongest sense you had around you at the time? Conviction of sin! People began to confess publicly what you might call "big sin." They spoke of adultery, cheating, stealing, and deceit. One friend, whom I thought too good to be true, was crying out to God for mercy and confessing her sins. I couldn't imagine she'd done anything wrong...There were also amazing visions of hell and people would break down weeping because of unsaved relatives. They carried exhausting prayer burdens. There were waves of outpoured prayer. Some went off at 4 AM on one occasion and walked twelve miles to a village, compelled by the Holy Spirit, to share the gospel. Many were saved as a result.[139]

REVELATION AFTER DEVASTATION

Revelation always follows devastation if we allow the Lord to have His way in our lives. Isaiah the prophet wrote, "In the year that King Uzziah died I saw the Lord sitting upon a throne, high and lifted up..."[140] Uzziah had been a great and prosperous King of Judah.[141] Yet, he ventured beyond his God-given authority when attempting to offer incense in the temple as only the priests were authorized to do.[142] His pride became his downfall.[143] Consequently, he was struck with leprosy and lived in seclusion until the day of his death.[144]

138 Hughes S. Why Revival Waits. Nashville, TN: Broadman & Holman Publishers; 2003.
139 Revival in the Congo! Jesus Army. ...Complete footnote: francisanfuso.com/awakened
140 Isaiah 6:1, ESV
141 2Chronicles 26:3–15
142 2Chronicles 26:16–21
143 2Chronicles 26:16
144 2Chronicles 26:21

As a young man in this king's court, Isaiah had the highest respect for the mighty and successful king. But Uzziah's rebellion caused a terrible season of disillusionment for Isaiah. Finally, when the king died in disgrace, Isaiah was jolted awake and set onto a journey leading to a heavenly relationship with God. In a vision, he saw the Lord surrounded by angelic beings called seraphim, "Above him stood the seraphim. Each had six wings: with two he covered his face, and with two he covered his feet, and with two he flew. And one called to another and said: 'Holy, holy, holy is the LORD of hosts; the whole earth is full of his glory!'"[145]

This verse demonstrates a key fact. If the seraphim who abide in the presence of the most holy God must shield their faces, how much more should we, in our fallen state, humble ourselves before Him. Isaiah then cried out, "Woe is me! For I am lost; for I am a man of unclean lips, and I dwell in the midst of a people of unclean lips; for my eyes have seen the King, the LORD of hosts! Then one of the seraphim flew to me, having in his hand a burning coal that he had taken with tongs from the altar. And he touched my mouth and said: 'Behold, this has touched your lips; your guilt is taken away, and your sin atoned for.'"[146]

To be overwhelmed by the presence of God is not an overreaction. When John, the closest disciple to Jesus, was taken up in the Spirit and encountered King Jesus enthroned above, he "...fell at His feet as dead."[147]

God's presence is always humbling.

Isaiah's experience likewise transformed him. Once he acknowledged his sinfulness, God invited the prophet into a profound relationship. "And I heard the voice of the Lord saying, 'Whom shall I send, and who will go for us?' Then I said, 'Here am I! Send me.'"[148]

---

145 Isaiah 6:2–3, ESV
146 Isaiah 6:5–7, ESV
147 Revelation 1:17, NKJV
148 Isaiah 6:8, ESV

Suddenly, Isaiah was ready for his next assignment: prophesy to the nation; and receive a glimpse of the coming Messiah. We must realize that the same holiness that killed Uzziah cleansed Isaiah. It remains a constant. We become part of the move of God only when we are cleansed and humbled, and that follows repentance. Uzziah was humbled by his circumstances. In contrast, Isaiah took the initiative and humbled himself before God. Consequently he was the one God set apart for His purposes.

Jesus fills only those who hunger and thirst.

The greater the hunger is, the greater the revival will be. The lesser our thirst is for God to move the less He will move. When the "...prince of the power of the air..." is finally cast down, and the breath of God fills our spirits, souls, and bodies, then we will at last become what God intended—His fully surrendered sons and daughters.[149]

PRAYER FOR GIFT OF REPENTANCE

"Father God, even though I have failed, You have not created me to be a failure. You bore my failures in Your broken body when You died in my place. Give me faith to receive Your gift of repentance and forgiveness, to rise above the failures of yesterday, and to joyfully anticipate the victories of tomorrow.

"Lord Jesus, wear down the resistance of my heart until I am completely surrendered. Give me this gift of repentance, that I too may no longer tolerate the intolerable and accept the unacceptable. Let me be wholly Yours! For You have conquered my sin, spared me from death, and purchased my life with Your precious blood. In Jesus name, Amen!"

---

149 Ephesians 2:2, ESV

PRAYER CONFESSION BY CHARLES SPURGEON

"I am not affected by the death of Jesus as I ought to be, neither am I moved by the ruin of my fellow men, the wickedness of the times, the chastisement of my heavenly Father, and my own failures, as I should be. O that my heart would melt at the recital of my Savior's sufferings and death.... Blessed be the name of the Lord, the disease is not incurable, the Savior's precious blood is the universal solvent, and me, even me, it will effectually soften, until my heart melts as wax before the fire."

QUESTIONS FOR GROUP DISCUSSION

1. Have you ever repented of your sins before God? If so, was this repentance a significant experience for you? Please describe.

2. Do you believe that you can and should be more willing to acknowledge your sin before others in order to activate the grace and power of God?

3. Have you ever been in a group where people genuinely confessed their sins and you sensed the presence of God?

4. What keeps you from acknowledging your sin before God and others?

5. How can you make repentance a lifestyle instead of an occasional event?

CHAPTER 4: SUPERNATURAL SURPRISES

Everything about a genuine revival from God is supernatural.

From preaching to praying, manifestations to mysteries, the entire affair goes beyond natural order. God is its author and finisher. As "in the beginning God created" so too the Creator revives what is dead or dormant.[150] He delights in breathing life into dry bones.[151] The chief architect and conductor of Heaven comes to Earth.

Perhaps this explains why revivals are controversial at times. God shows up in ways that often cause outsiders to think some folks are either drunk or crazy.[152] Having been saved in a revival myself—The Jesus Movement—I can tell you the event was anything but commonplace. On the morning of my salvation, I didn't wake up thinking, "Today is the day I receive Jesus and everlasting life."

When I invited Him to be Lord of my life, I experienced a convergence of the human, heavenly, and demonic realms. I prayed, "Jesus, I don't know if You are who that man says You are, but, if You are, do for me what You did for him." At that exact moment, a remarkable surprise occurred. Both the Japa beads representing the Hindu deity, Krishna, and the turquoise strand that supposedly communicated with Venusians (people from the

150 Genesis 1:1, NKJV
151 Ezekiel 37:1–14
152 Acts 2:16

planet Venus) began to choke me.[153] I, of course, didn't realize that both objects had demonic associations.

Feeling strangled, I prayed a desperate second prayer—"Jesus help me!" At that climactic moment, my frozen hands were suddenly released, and I ripped the necklaces off. I gasped for breath while hundreds of beads scattered on the floor. In a moment my life had been transformed. The first two weeks of my newfound faith I devoured half of the New Testament exhausting everyone around me with countless questions.

Revival had come to my life. But not just to me. In many places during that unique window in time, people were suddenly coming to Jesus. The year was 1972. The Jesus Movement ushered perhaps as many as 3 million primarily young people from 70 countries into the Kingdom of God.

The birth of the Church was no different. The first supernatural surprise in the New Testament Church happened "suddenly." The book of Acts states, "suddenly there came from heaven..."[154]

Unexpectedly and without warning, Heaven came to Earth. That's revival!

SUPERNATURAL SURPRISES

Since the glorious day of Pentecost, the Spirit of God has sprung supernatural surprises upon unsuspecting people. He overtakes, revolutionizes, and thrills them. Without exception, God releases supernatural power to redeem that which the church lacks.

Charles Spurgeon said, "Revival is a season of glorious disorder."

Duncan Campbell, the revivalist who helped birth the Hebridean Revival of 1949, states it this way, "Of the hundreds who found Jesus Christ at that time, seventy-five percent were gloriously saved before they came near a meeting, before they heard a single sermon...the power of God was moving, the Spirit of God was in operation, and the fear of God gripping the souls of men."[155]

---

153 Don't put the book down, you're almost finished with it. I'm doing a lot better now 40 years later!
154 Acts 2:2, ESV
155 The Lewis Revival, by Duncan Campbell of the ...Complete footnote: francisanfuso.com/awakened

Speaking of this move of God, Campbell said, "A Christian is a supernatural being who has had a supernatural experience..."[156]

George Whitefield, a catalyst for the First Great Awakening of the early 1700s, spoke to as many as 10 million people. During some of his meetings, people would cry out and fall to the ground under the supernatural conviction of God. Sean Smith shares,

> Great revivalists and theologians like Jonathan Edwards have realized that when God pours out His Spirit in power, it will look different from our norm, precisely because our norm is the problem. We need a new norm, and that's what revival comes to do. When a seriously strong presence of the Holy Spirit manifests, He will bring a conviction and otherworldly atmosphere that often affects one's emotions and physical body. Falling prostrate and shaking are mentioned in many revival accounts, but the key must be the fruit of a transformed life and Jesus as the central obsession.[157]

In the 18th century, Christmas Evans sparked a Welsh Revival.

> Thousands were saved as the power of God shook the country. People were so affected by his preaching that they broke out and literally danced for joy. As a result, they were called the 'Welsh Jumpers.' Others said the people seemed like the inhabitants of a city shaken by an earthquake; they would rush into the streets, falling upon the ground, screaming and calling upon God.[158]

In the Cane Ridge Revival of 1801, 20,000 people attended a six-day camp meeting on the American Frontier. A firsthand account is most revealing:

> The noise was like the roar of Niagara. The vast sea of human beings seemed to be agitated as if by a storm. I counted seven ministers, all preaching at one time, some on stumps, others in wagons and one standing on a tree...Some of the people were singing, others praying, some crying for mercy in the most piteous accents, while others were shouting most vociferously. While witnessing these scenes, a peculiar strange sensation such as I had

---

156 Campbell D. The Price and Power of Revival. Christian Literature Crusade; 1962.
157 Smith S. I Am Your Sign. Destiny Image, Inc.; 2011.
158 ibid.

never felt before came over me. My heart beat tumultuously, my knees trembled, my lips quivered and I felt as though I must fall to the ground. A strange supernatural power seemed to pervade the entire mass of mind there collected...I stepped up on a log where I could have a better view of the surging sea of humanity. The scene that then presented itself to my mind was indescribable. At one time I saw at least five hundred swept down in a moment as if a battery of a thousand guns had been opened upon them and immediately followed shrieks and shouts that rent the very heavens."[159]

Perhaps no evangelist or revivalist had more lasting fruit then Charles Finney. "Over eighty-five in every hundred persons professing conversion to Christ in Finney's meetings remained true to God. Finney seems to have had the power of impressing the conscience with the necessity of holy living in such a manner as to procure the most lasting results."[160]

When Finney went to Rome, New York, God so seized the folks with genuine conviction that Finney was concerned that the people couldn't control their emotions. He tried to be extra calm in the altar prayer, but the crowd had begun to convulse violently. Revival services went on for three weeks with people running to attend; ministers came from nearby towns to experience what was going on. So many people got saved in these services, in homes, and in businesses that it was impossible to keep up. Some mockers would get drunk all day and condemn the revival, until one of them fell down dead. After that, nearly all of the adult population of Rome was brought into the Kingdom. It was said that everyone who came to Rome felt an overwhelming sense of God's presence."[161]

There have also been lesser-known moves of God that are no less supernatural or surprising. In between the 1904 Welsh Revival and the 1906 Los Angeles Revival God moved in many places across the U.S. "In 1905, the ministers Association of Atlantic City, New Jersey reported that out of a population of 60,000 people

159 Mendell T. *Exploring Evangelism*. Beacon Hill Press; 1964.
160 From Deeper Experiences of Famous Christians ...Complete footnote: francisanfuso.com/awakened
161 Smith S. *I Am Your Sign*. Destiny Image, Inc.; 2011.

there were only 50 adults left unconverted. In Portland, Oregon during 1905, two hundred stores closed from 11AM to 2PM each day for prayer."[162]

Author J. Edwin Orr wrote of the 1905–1906 spiritual awakening in India:

- its sudden appearance...and disappearance
- its manifestation among believers
- its deep conviction of sin and repentance
- its laughter, joy, and singing that followed the realization of forgiveness
- its visions, trances and manifestations related to Christ's suffering on the cross

The principle leader of the *Azusa Street Revival* of 1906 was William Seymour, an African-American man born to former slaves. The Pentecostal Movement he helped launch has currently over 600 million adherents worldwide. At the height of the revival, Seymour would simply declare sick and disabled people in various parts of the room healed in the name of Jesus, and they would be.

Revival walks hand-in-hand with the supernatural, which is why it stirs exceptional faith in some and skepticism in others.

A SKEPTIC'S EYEWITNESS ACCOUNT OF REVIVAL

William T. Stead, the editor of the famous Pall Mall Gazette, was thought by some to be the most powerful man in Britain at the time of the Welsh Revival in 1904. He made a personal visit to the revival in Wales and recorded the following interview:

"A revival is something like a revolution. It is apt to be wonderfully catching."

"You speak as if you dreaded the revival coming your way," Said the interviewer.

"No. That is not so. Dread is not the right word. Awe expresses my sentiment better, for you are in the presence of the unknown. You have read ghost stories and can imagine what you would feel if you

---

162 Orr JE. Introduction to Revival. Retrieved from http://www.jedwinorr.com/audio.htm on June 12, 2012.

were alone at midnight in the haunted chamber of some old castle and you heard the slow and stealthy step stealing along the corridor where the visitor from another world was said to walk."

"If you go to South Wales and watch the revival, you will feel pretty much just like that. There is something there from the other world. You cannot say whence it came or whither it is going, but it moves and lives and reaches for you all the time. You see men and women go down in sobbing agony before your eyes as the invisible Hand clutches at their heart. And you shudder. It is pretty grim I tell you, if you are afraid of strong emotions, you'd better give the revival a wide berth."[163]

Years later Stead would die as a passenger on the Titanic.

REVIVAL MINEFIELDS

Beyond the menagerie of divisions that threaten the existence and continuance of revivals, lie mines of immorality, unethical financial practices, and spiritual deception that litter the harvest fields.

In the Introduction of this book I mentioned that I had reviewed great books about revival I've read over the years. I realized afresh that grave danger beset the most powerful revivals in church history before, during, and after their arrival. My findings were so disconcerting that, in prayer before the Lord, I honestly considered if I was indeed willing to face these potential hazards.

Though my answer was yes, I resolved that I would alert those pursuing revival to the minefields connected with such a grand undertaking. The mother of all dangers to revival is *division*. Perhaps that's why it's one of the seven things the Lord hates, "a person who sows discord in a family"[164] There is no family more important to God than His own—the Body of Christ.

Throughout the history of the church, fellow believers invariably attempt to discredit true revivals for two reasons. Either they disagree with the leader's methods or they believe their method of promoting revival would be better.

163 Shaw SB. *The Great Revival in Wales.* Etherington Conservation Services; 2006.
164 Proverbs 6:19, NLT

Here are two historical examples.

Welsh Revival: During the Welsh Revival of 1904, a nationally famous Welsh preacher, Peter Price, denounced Evan Roberts, the revival's principal protagonist, and his methods, as false, shallow, and unreal. However, Price considered his own methods genuine and said as much both publicly and in print. This so devastated Roberts that he withdrew from ministry altogether and never again ministered in public. "He rejected all callers, ignored all letters, and even refused to see his own concerned family. After this he only emerged rarely at some public religious events, usually unnoticed and unheralded, and to all but a few who remembered, was essentially forgotten."[165]

Azusa Street Revival: William Seymour, the spearhead of the Pentecostal Revival of 1906 in Los Angeles, was a humble man. One who knew him well said:

> *He is the meekest man I have ever met. He walks and talks with God. His power is in his weakness. He seems to maintain a helpless dependence upon God, and is as simple-hearted as a little child. And at the same time so filled with God you feel the love and power every time you get near him.*[166]

Seymour was a Bible student of Charles Parham. Seymour was black and Parham was white and a strict segregationist who erroneously believed that to mix the races was unbiblical. Both men were disturbed by disingenuous manifestations seen during the revival, but Seymour believed uprooting the fake from the real would quench the Spirit. He chose to let the wheat and the weeds grow up together.[167]

The mixing of races and the diversity of manifestations offended Parham to the extent that he started a rival group across town. Even though it failed to make an impact, Parham spent the remainder of his life denouncing Seymour and the Azusa Street Revival, losing both followers and influence until his death in 1929.

165 Pratney W. *Revival.* Createspace; 2010.
166 Apostolic Faith, February/March 1907, Testimony ...Complete footnote: francisanfuso.com/awakened
167 Matthew 13:29–30

The minefields of revival are inevitable. We must therefore heed the Biblical admonition: "Be sober-minded; be watchful. Your adversary the devil prowls around like a roaring lion, seeking someone to devour."[168] Be ever on guard, "...so that Satan will not outsmart us. For we are familiar with his evil schemes."[169]

JOY AND TEARS IN REVIVAL

Revival. There are so many misconceptions about this word. Is revival a morbid experience for hyper-melancholies or an over-used advertisement describing nothing more than spiritual excess? Neither! True revival is a move of God. It is God pouring Himself upon people to revive His own and awaken the lost. Is revival tearful or joyful? Both! The revivals recorded in the Old Testament demonstrated a sincere repentance of sin followed by great joy and gladness. Throughout church history, all of the great revivalists could cry one minute and laugh the next. When the Israelites returned to rebuild the temple in Jerusalem, after having been slaves in Babylon for 70 years this was clearly the case. "But many of the priests and Levites and heads of fathers' houses, old men who had seen the first house, wept with a loud voice when they saw the foundation of this house being laid, though many shouted aloud for joy..."[170]

British author, Dr. Martyn-Lloyd Jones writes, "That is what happens in revival and thus you get this curious, strange mixture, as it were, of great conviction of sin and great joy, a great sense of the terror of the Lord, and great thanksgiving and praise. Always in a revival there is what somebody once called a divine disorder. Some are groaning and agonizing under conviction, others praising God for the great salvation. And all this leads to crowded and prolonged meetings. Time seems to be forgotten. People seem to have entered into eternity."[171]

---

168 1Peter 5:8, ESV
169 2Corinthians 2:11, NLT
170 Ezra 3:12, ESV
171 Jones, ML. What is Revival? Retrieved from ...Complete footnote: francisanfuso.com/awakened

This contrast was evident in both evangelists and revivalists. Charles Spurgeon, the prince of preachers, possessed a contagious joy. His sense of humor was renowned.

The revivals recorded in the Old Testament demonstrated a sincere repentance of sin followed by great joy and gladness. Throughout church history, all of the great revivalists could cry one minute and laugh the next.

The great evangelist, D.L. Moody, who led as many as one million people to Jesus, could never speak of a lost soul without tearful eyes.

George Whitefield preached sermons filled with pathos. He commonly wept from the pulpit. One person who often traveled to hear him speak said he had not seen him deliver a message without a tear. Even those who came with hostility toward Whitefield could not hate a man who wept so much over their souls. "I came to hear you with a pocket full of stones to break your head," said one convert, "but your sermon got the better of me, and God broke my heart."

During the Welsh Revival, the dominant note of the revival was prayer and praise. Its primary leader, Evan Roberts, was a man filled with joy. To the typical church leader of his day, this was his most incomprehensible quality. They considered their Christian faith "hyper-serious, severe—even terrible. Evan Roberts smiled when he prayed and laughed when he preached." He gladdened those around him with, "Ah, it is a grand life! I am happy, so happy that I could walk on air. Tired? Never. God has made me strong. He has given me courage." Evan preached and embodied victory and showed how it could be won. His view of God was a welcome departure from the depressing religion of his day. Evan wrote, "God is a happy God and a joyful God. Therefore, we must be happy and joyful. Now, when we speak of religion we are full of joy, and our faces are lit up with joy. Shake off this death-like solemnity, and be joyful, ever joyful. We must show the world that we are happy, because of this blessed assurance of salvation."[173]

---

172 Pratney W. *Revival.* Createspace; 2010.

173 Adams K. *The Diary of Revival.* Crusade for World Revival; 2004.

Two days before the Welsh Revival began, a church service took place where:

> *Almost everyone in attendance...was moved to tears. Many cried in agony. By midnight the presence of the Lord was so intense that it could hardly be contained. The people had never experienced such a deep repentance or such deep joy. Those crying in remorse for their sins could not be distinguished from those crying in ecstasy at the nearness of God. It was after 3 am before an attempt to close the meeting was possible.*[174]

One newspaper's account read: "The scene is almost indescribable. Prayer after prayer went up… A policeman, who came to complain that the people had gone so mad after religion that there was nothing for him to do, burst into tears, confessed the error of his ways, and repented."

Perhaps here is the secret of true revival: we cannot merely pray for it, we must repent of all sin, give our all to God, and welcome His sudden and supernatural move in our lives. May we experience the joy of seeing the Church that Jesus loves revived, and the lost He died for awakened.

PRAYER FOR SUPERNATURAL SURPRISES:

"Jesus, You lived a supernaturally natural life while here on Earth, choosing to do nothing in Your own strength, but only what You saw Your Father doing and relying on His power. It is the way I want to live, though I often fall far short of this goal.

"Prepare my heart to obey the sudden lines You have written in Your script for me. I know that they are designed to make me the person You created me to be. Please give me the courage to step out boldly in supernatural realms when You lead me to. I want to walk in complete faith believing that Your Word and promises are true and can be fully relied upon even when, in the natural, they may seem impossible."

---

174 Joyner R. *The Power To Change The World*...Complete footnote: francisanfuso.com/awakened

QUESTIONS FOR GROUP DISCUSSION

1. Do you know anyone who was saved in a supernatural revival? If so, what did they share about it with you?

2. Has God been stirring your heart to believe for a revival of His Spirit in your own life and those you love?

3. Would you be open and excited to see God move supernaturally in the way described in this chapter? Please explain.

4. Does the thought of revival stir skepticism or faith in you? Why?

5. What fears might you have about revival coming to your own life and church? What revival "minefields" concern you the most?

CHAPTER FIVE: SELFLESS SERVING

"If sinners will be damned let them perish with our arms about their knees, if hell is to be filled, let no one go there unloved or unprayed for. I would be willing to die if I could be honored bringing one sinner to Jesus."

—Charles Haddon Spurgeon

Have you ever heard of John Staupitz, Edward Kimball, or John Egglen?

Not really household names, are they?

John Staupitz was a little known monk who led the legendary reformer Martin Luther to Christ.

Edward Kimball was a shoe salesman and Sunday school teacher who led the great evangelist D.L. Moody to the Lord.

John Egglen was a deacon in a Methodist church who had never preached a sermon until the Sunday he invited the future prince of preachers, Charles Spurgeon, to surrender his life to Jesus.

What was the name of the woman at the well, the little boy with loaves and fishes, the woman with an alabaster box, or the widow with two mites? God loves to use nameless, faceless people.

Though they were nameless, faceless people, they were legendary!

Such is the role of a servant. Many who make headlines on Earth are legends in the minds of man, whereas servants make headlines in Heaven and are legends in the heart of God. Jesus said, "whoever would be first among you must be your slave..."[175] God "made himself nothing, taking the form of a servant, being born in the likeness of men. And being found in human form, he humbled himself by becoming obedient to the point of death, even death on a cross."[176]

All of us who claim to be Christ's followers are called to be servants. Only in serving others do we truly represent our humble Creator well. Revivals birthed in the heart of God must find residence in the souls of praying men and women—those willing to pay the price of selflessly serving their generation, not with mere words, but with actions, replicating the love of God. God's Word must always be accompanied with His authentic works. This was the original acid test for the first followers of Christ. After Jesus commissioned them, "they went out and preached everywhere, the Lord working with them and confirming the word through the accompanying signs."[177]

May Jesus confirm His Word in and through us with works that reflect Him well.

A SERVING HEART

Jesus commanded: "love one another as I have loved you. Greater love has no one than this, that someone lays down his life for his friends."[178] It is in laying down our lives for others that we are most Christ-like.

By age 12, Evan Roberts worked in the coalmines where he remained for 12 years. During this time he joined one of the mine's rescue teams. Rescuing others became a high priority throughout his entire life. Twice during their childhood Evan rescued his younger brother Dan from certain death—once from drowning, and another time when Dan had fallen into a well.

---

175 Matthew 20:27, ESV
176 Philippians 2:7–8, ESV
177 Mark 16:20, NKJV
178 John 15:12b–13, ESV

Evan also saved a friend from a violent stream, even though— at that time—Evan was unable to swim himself.

A childhood friend said of Evan Roberts, "He was one of the most wise, most fair of judgment, most easygoing and kind of all that I came to know as a child." Daniel Phillips wrote what is considered the standard biography on the life of Evan Roberts.

He was a minister and frequent companion to Evan on many of his journeys. From his writings we spot a glimpse into the life of the man God used to spearhead perhaps the greatest revival since the first century.

To get a first-hand account of Evan's personal character, Phillips interviewed someone who worked alongside him in the coalmines and, for a season, lived with him. Evan's friend shared that as a worker, in order to help others, he consistently gravitated toward the most challenging tasks. He sympathized with those having difficulty. It gave Evan great pleasure to help a friend or a co-worker, and he didn't grow weary, even when asked to help over and over again. It was—therefore—no accident that during the great revival, Evan worked tirelessly to serve God by helping people in need.

The Bible outlines perhaps the loftiest of all goals: "Do nothing from selfishness or empty conceit, but with humility of mind *regard one another as more important than yourselves*; do not merely look out for your own personal interests, but also for the interests of others."[179] What a challenge!

When it comes to loving others, would the God who is love exaggerate? Would He overstate how we should treat one another? Does God really want us to esteem others as more important, more significant, even better than ourselves? Perhaps our willingness to yield to God's Spirit in this way will determine if we will ever see a genuine move of God in our lifetime.

---

179 Philippians 2:3–4, NASB

SONS OR SERVANTS

Though God has created us to serve, we are called to be sons and daughters who serve, not slaves who serve. The basic difference between a son or daughter and a servant is relationship. Do you have a stake in the family of God? Servants serve, and sons and daughters serve, but only sons and daughters will inherit. It has everything to do with our attitude or motive for serving.

If serving others ultimately serves our own benefit, then we have made ourselves a slave. If, on the other hand, serving is for the glory of God and to bless other members of His family, then we serve with the heart of Jesus. He made Himself a servant so we could become sons and daughters. "And because you are sons, God has sent forth the Spirit of His Son into your hearts, crying out, 'Abba, Father!' Therefore you are no longer a slave but a son, and if a son, then an heir of God through Christ."[180]

Many people have a "disposable relationship" mentality. It goes something like this: I'll be connected to you as long as you are meeting a need I have. Its motive is not to give and serve but to take and use others. The Bible refers to this as being a "hireling" or a "hired hand."[181,182] I'm here for a paycheck. If there's nothing in it for me, then I'm out. How many sons and daughters have broken hearts because parents ditched their nurturing role? An even more tragic condition is that, unless we break the pattern of abandonment, we repeat it in our own relationships.

Frankly, without commitment and ownership we have no future, no safety, and no security. Jesus said, "He who is a hired hand and not a shepherd, who does not own the sheep, sees the wolf coming and leaves the sheep and flees, and the wolf snatches them and scatters them."[183]

If a store catches fire, a paid employee may just leave, but an owner will stay and fight the flames. Sons and daughters stay and fight. Sons and daughters know if the family goes down, they go

180 Galatians 4:6–7, NKJV
181 John 10:12, KJV
182 John 10:12, ESV
183 ibid.

down. If the family's reputation gets soiled, their reputation gets muddied.

Now comes the ultimate significance of this principle. We who name the name of Jesus, who claim to be His sons and daughters, either model His servant heart or distort His flawless name and reputation. Haven't we all seen how quickly others hold us to the highest standard imaginable when we say that we are followers of Jesus? It is because deep down people realize that Jesus embodies everything good and pure and just—all that we could ever hope to be.

PREMATURE RETIREMENT

Too many rescued men and women of God have gone into early retirement. We have put ourselves out to pasture. The fire that once burned hot to live for Jesus has grown cold. Either we allow God to rekindle it, or we will become one of history's "has-beens"—a shell of our potential. Starting out hot, we have nestled into lukewarmness. Have we bowed to apathy and indifference, and missed the sublime identity and destiny God had prepared uniquely for each of us?

When it comes to giving, some people stop at nothing. Literally!

When it comes to giving, God gives His first and best, the cream off the top. "God so loved the world that He gave His only begotten Son, that whoever believes in Him should not perish but have everlasting life."[184] It will always take the most faith to give your best. That's why God's Word tells us, "without faith it is impossible to please God."[185] Faith gets God's attention. Only God knows the true value of all things; He knows how much living in genuine faith will cost.

There's nothing in the world that's more impressive than the heart of a giver. It is a rare sighting! When we are fortunate enough to see it, we catch a glimpse into the very nature of God. Giving away what you don't need isn't giving; it's liquidation—a garage sale. It

---

184 John 3:16, NKJV
185 Hebrews 11:6, NIV

takes faith to obediently give what you think you need, so that God can give you what He knows you really need.

Selflessly giving—one of the most Christ-like behaviors—frees God's Spirit to flow in us. Paul quoted Jesus when he said, "It is more blessed—makes one happier and more to be envied—to give than to receive."[186] Jesus is a giver, and He's looking for people who want to be like Him! He created us to be rivers of giving, not stagnant ponds. How do you know if you're a giver? It's simple! When God asks you to give to someone or something, you respond positively and are even excited to obey Him. You have a giving mentality. If, on the other hand, you think, "I don't have enough to give and obey God," then your mindset is impoverished.

Each of our lives has three dimensions from which we can give: our time, talents and treasures. It is within these three areas that we struggle to obey God. It is also in these areas that we come to see how truly prosperous we are.

God longs for us to prosper, but He cannot grant prosperity beyond the limits of our soul. Frankly, we couldn't handle it. He longs for us to know Him and reflect Him to others. As our soul longs for Jesus, our boundaries for blessings expand. For this reason John, the beloved disciple, wrote, "I pray that you may prosper in all things and be in health, just as your soul prospers."[187]

Many of us are waiting for God to bless our lives.

He patiently waits for us to give Him something deserving His blessing.

HEAVEN COMES TO EARTH

How will we know when Heaven comes to Earth?

When we see God, the Servant King, bring redemption to the undeserving, joy to the gloomy, and rest to the weary, we will witness Heaven's glory.

---

186 Acts 20:35, AMP
187 3John 1:2, NKJV

We have all been slaves of sin. Many of us during our slave years held others captive as well. I remember the people I persuaded to indulge in drugs and those I robbed of moral purity. But I also know that "God saved a wretch like me..."

So why do so many of us continue as slaves instead of sons? God does not desire to humiliate us. He will honor us after we have voluntarily humbled ourselves. Rick Warren says it simply. "Humility is not thinking less of yourself; it's thinking of yourself less."[188]

Before we live in Heaven, may Heaven live in us!

The Reverend Martin Luther King Jr. said, "Everybody can be great, because everybody can serve. You don't have to have a college degree to serve. You don't have to make your subject and verb agree to serve. You only need a heart full of grace. A soul generated by love."[189] One of the great joys in life is serving others.

We know Heaven has come when we *love* like our Creator, *serve* like our Creator, and *honor* like our Creator.

Loving and serving even those who hate and abuse is the call of all true Christians. It is in our future! Paul, the persecuted Apostle, wrote: "We serve God whether people honor us or despise us, whether they slander us or praise us. We are honest, but they call us impostors."[190]

The founder of the Children's Defense Fund, Marian Wright Edelman, states, "Service is the rent we each pay for living. It is not something to do in your spare time; it is the very purpose of life."[191] Serving, as defined by the Bible, is found in Jesus. "... whoever desires to become great among you, let him be your servant. And whoever desires to be first among you, let him be your slave—just as the Son of Man did not come to be served [to be waited on], but to serve, and to give His life a ransom for many."[192]

---

188 GoodQuotes.com. Rick Warren Quotes. 2010. ... Complete footnote: francisanfuso.com/awakened
189 Martin Luther King, Jr.
190 2Corinthians 6:8a, NLT
191 Marian Wright Edelman, Founder ... Complete footnote: francisanfuso.com/awakened
192 Matthew 20:26b–28, NKJV

Why do so few people hit the mark of selfless serving? Because they aim too low! C.S. Lewis said, "Aim at Heaven and you will get Earth thrown in. Aim at Earth and you get neither."

I'm pursuing the sonship only an Eternal Father could offer.

I'm aiming for Heaven!

EVERYONE LOVES

Everyone loves! We can't help ourselves. That's how we're wired. Hermits love solitude. Misers love money. Addicts love addictions. Pundits love opinions. We can see that what we love speaks directly to who we are. Because "God is love" what we love also determines whether or not we love God.[193]

Do we love what God loves: people?

Do we love how God loves: unconditionally?

Jesus was wary of the religious leaders of His day. He was troubled by their "… desire to go around in long robes, love greetings in the marketplaces, the best seats in the synagogues, and the best places at feasts, who devour widows' houses, and for a pretense make long prayers. These will receive greater condemnation."[194] They loved the applause of men and pretended to have more of a relationship with God than they really had.

Do we do that? Do we pretend to *love* more than we do, *give* more than we do—*serve* more than we do, and *honor* more than we actually do? For better or worse, love will always be the acid test for authenticity. It qualifies our motives, judges our deeds, and is the tipping point for God's acceptance or rejection.

Why does God emphasize love?

Because "three things will last forever—faith, hope, and love—and the greatest of these is love."[195]

---

193 1John 4:8b, NKJV
194 Mark 12:38–40, NKJV
195 1Corinthians 13:13, NLT

Whenever and wherever the next awakening takes place, it is guaranteed that nameless and faceless vessels who selflessly love, give, serve, and honor one another will see Heaven once again touch Earth.

PRAYER FOR SELFLESS SERVANTS

"Father God, You selflessly sent Your Son to die a criminals death after living the life of a servant. As Your son, I submit my will, and ask that You give me a servant's heart as well. I know that my tendency is to gravitate to self-gratification rather than selflessly serving others. Please forgive me for this. It is not who I want to be.

"Lord Jesus, You came to serve, not be served. If You freely chose that lowly yet lofty position, I must do no less. Transform my selfish heart to reflect Yours. Let my motive for saying or doing anything be to please only You—for You know the true value of all my words and works. You are the God who lives to love, serve, and give selflessly to Your entire creation. Help me do the same."

QUESTIONS FOR GROUP DISCUSSION

1. Do you believe that your highest calling as a Christ follower is to serve?

2. How do you presently incorporate serving others into your own life?

3. Do you believe that loving and serving others is the most powerful way to demonstrate the heart of God?

4. What would happen if all followers of Jesus selflessly served those around them?

5. Do you believe that an extended season of serving others with the love of God would assist in awakening their hearts to Jesus?

CHAPTER SIX:
MAKING
DISCIPLES

There is no such thing as an undisciplined disciple.

To strip away a disciple's true identity will ultimately destroy his God-given destiny. As disciples of Jesus, we must first be disciplined learners in order to teach others. Jesus commissioned us to do no less when He said, "Go therefore and make disciples of all nations, teaching them to observe all that I have commanded you..."[196]

With this in mind, there are two essential aspects of revival to remember. Focusing on them sharpens and prepares us for God working in and through us.

1. Revivals rescue the next generation.

The harvest is always young! Journalist William Stead provides a riveting account of the principal audience of the Welsh Revival of 1904.

> *At all these meetings the same kind of thing went on — the same kind of congregations assembled, the same strained, intense emotion was manifest. Aisles were crowded. Pulpit stairs were packed and two-thirds of the congregation were men, and at least one-half young men. "There," said one, "is the hope and the glory of the movement." Here and there is a grey head. But the majority of*

196 Matthew 28:19, NKJV

the congregation were stalwart young miners, who gave the meeting all the fervour and swing and enthusiasm of youth.[197]

2. *Revivals are only as effective as the converts they disciple.*

As Evan Roberts prophesied just three weeks prior to the Welsh awakening of 1904, over one hundred thousand souls were saved within a year in Wales alone. It was a glorious beginning. But the harvest could perhaps have been more effective. Missionary and author, Norman Grubb provides, from his perspective, a revealing summation of the church's neglect before and after the move of God.

> *It is important to learn from the mistakes made during the Revival. Roberts was no expositor of the Word, and this was a weakness that was passed on to the new converts, who relied heavily on emotion and not upon Scripture. In a sense the revival was based upon the preaching of a previous generation of ministers and Sunday School teachers, whose efforts finally bore fruit in 1904. When the Revival began to decline the established churches found it difficult to disciple the new converts, which is what they desperately needed.*[198]

This is a tragic assessment that begs the following questions:

Are our churches ready to nurture and disciple the multitudes of new converts a move of God would birth into His Kingdom?

If not, dare we ask for such a move of God?

Perhaps we should contemplate this ultimate reality while praying for God to move.

Do we really believe a Biblically illiterate church would be capable of nurturing thousands of new believers? I'm persuaded it would not!

Yet, by contrast, many cults are! Groups like Jehovah's Witnesses and Mormons are very disciplined in methodically sharing their teachings, though tragically in error when it comes to the foundational doctrines of the Christian faith.

---

197 Stead W. *Daily Chronicle*. December 13, 1904.

198 Grubb N. *Rees Howells, Intercessor.* Fort Washington, PA: CLC Publications; 1983.

Perhaps God hesitates to awaken those we love knowing the church is unprepared to disciple them in His Word?

We think we are waiting for God to move, when in reality, *it's our move.*

REVIVALISTS, EVANGELISTS, AND PRESERVING THE HARVEST

As there are seasons of natural harvest on Earth, Heaven's harvest of eternal souls is seasonal as well. During the planting, watering, and pre-harvest seasons of reaching the lost, the two primary tillers and planters of the spiritual ground are the *revivalist* and the *evangelist.*

A *revivalist* spearheads a revival. He or she believes it in, prays it in, and preaches it in. Revivalists like Jonathan Edwards, Evan Roberts, and Charles Finney couldn't be more different in personality and background. Yet, when they arrived at the intersection of Heaven and Earth, they became the catalysts God used to start a holy fire.

An *evangelist*, on the other hand, is someone who preaches the gospel that establishes a revival. Evangelists George Whitefield, John Wesley, and D. L. Moody recognized the initial flames and began gathering the eternal souls that were ready to surrender to Jesus. As in the case of Charles Finney, some function in both roles and may be considered both revivalists and evangelists.

Evangelists and revivalists don't start revivals. Revivals start them! Wesley, Whitefield, Finney, Moody, and Philip of the Book of Acts couldn't impart anything lasting on Earth until they were empowered with everything eternal from Heaven.

Church leaders should not feel threatened when a revival comes to their city. More often than not, every supportive church will be filled to overflowing with new converts. As was the case with Simon who fished all night and caught nothing, when Jesus showed up, there came with Him a mighty harvest, "they caught so many fish that their nets were beginning to break."[199]

---

199 Luke 5:6, NRSV

Revivals often transcend denominations and church groups though some individual churches have openly opposed them. In 1905, as the Welsh revival spread across the United States, "Everyone was so busy in Chicago that pastors decided to hold their own meeting and help one another deal with the influx."[200]

But the true value of any revival is in the transformed lives of those converted and planted in local churches. Finney's revivals in New York State in the 1830s may reflect such merit. As many as 80 percent of new converts were established in churches. The same is true for the Welsh Revival of 1904 in which 75 percent of those converted became connected to a local church.

WHITEFIELD'S GREAT AWAKENING REVIVAL

God used George Whitefield as the principle evangelist to fire up the First Great Awakening in American history during the early 1700s. Fifty thousand people or twenty percent of the population of New England were added to the churches.[201]

As a boy, George Whitefield bullied, lied, stole, and gambled. As a teenager, he mocked preachers from bar stools. Once, he even got drunk and, with his friends, broke up a church meeting.

Yet, as a converted adult, he ministered to multitudes that came to know Jesus. Whitefield's sermons were filled with immense feeling.

When Whitefield later returned to America, his ministry impacted even the skeptic Benjamin Franklin. Franklin declared, "It seems as all the world is growing religious." Because of Whitefield's powerful and expressive voice, it was said that on a clear day you could hear him for five miles!

For the next thirty years he traversed the Atlantic preaching 18,000 messages to crowds as large as 30,000 people. One renowned cynic called Whitefield, "the most extraordinary man in our times." He obtained a degree of popularity such as no preacher before or since has probably ever reached.

200 Orr JE. The Re-Study of Revival and Revivalism, 1981.
201 Waugh G. *Fire Fell: Revival Visitations*. Brisbane: Renewal. Australia.

From Whitefield, we learn this: God can use anyone who utterly devotes himself to God and to loving His people.

WESLEY'S METHODIST REVIVAL

John Wesley, founder of Methodism, was an anointed revivalist with lasting fruit. At the time of his death, 88,000 Christians declared themselves Methodists.[202] While history records Wesley's failure to nurture his own family, the fruits of his ministry are worthy of note. Here are some of John Wesley's own words, which provide a short summary of Methodism's origin, and I believe the secret of his effectiveness in relational small groups.

Wesley wrote:

> *They were all zealous members of the Church of England; not only tenacious of all her doctrines, so far as they knew them, but of all her discipline, to the minutest circumstance...But they observed neither these nor anything else any further than they conceived it was bound upon them by their one book, the Bible; it being their one desire and design to be downright Bible-Christians...[203]*

In November of 1729, four students from Oxford University, which included John and Charles Wesley, "began to spend some evenings in a week together, in reading, chiefly, the Greek Testament." Over the next few years, other students joined, one of which was the great evangelist George Whitefield, who began attending in 1735. They were so faithful and disciplined in meeting that the name "Methodists" was soon attached to them.

John Wesley left England in 1735 to preach in America, but it wasn't until his return to England in 1738, when he read Luther's preface to the *Epistle to the Romans*, that he was truly converted. He became convinced, "that 'by grace we are saved through faith;' that justification by faith was the doctrine of the Church, as well as of the Bible."[204]

---

202 Blumhofer EL, Balmer R. *Modern Christian Revivals*. University of Illinois Press; 1993.
203 Wesley J. *A Short History of Methodism*. ... Complete footnote: francisanfuso.com/awakened
204 ibid.

Wesley's conviction to gather small clusters of believers to study the Bible and be relationally connected was a return to Christ's example. Jesus Himself gathered and prepared the first disciples to lead the fledgling church in His absence.

WESLEY'S SOCIAL EXPERIMENT

A significant aspect of the ministry of Jesus was built on a small group model. It provided *relationship, instruction and accountability*. The early disciples shared their lives and faith in community. This is the New Testament pattern for healthy growth and discipleship for all believers.

John Wesley believed that in order to live a holy life it was necessary for followers of Jesus to regularly share their lives in intimate fellowship with one another. His 18th century small groups revolutionized England.

Wesley structured instruction and accountability into three sections: *Societies, Classes,* and *Bands.*

- *Societies* focused on education. In a large classroom setting, doctrine was taught through preaching, reading the Word, worship and exhortation. Attendees listened to lectures but did not interact. Initially, ordained clergy led the meetings. In time, lay men and women were equipped to lead.

- *Classes* focused on influence through relationship. Consisting of 10 to 12 people in intimate weekly gatherings, they helped supervise an individual's spiritual growth. Classes, which included women, were a mixed bag of spiritual maturity, social status, and age. Wesley wanted to represent a cross section of the church in order to break down the rigid social structure of 18th century England. In transparent environments, leaders shared openly about their struggles, failures, sins, temptations, and spiritual battles. They centered on personal life experiences, not doctrinal or Biblical truth. Sharing hearts in love was the goal of each class meeting. A leader's vulnerability created trust for others to share honestly as well. Consequently, the class affected a significant level of mutual support to help others live holy and victorious lives.

- *Bands* focused on direction. Homogeneous groups based on age, gender and marital status committed to honesty and transparency at a deeper level. Those attending were encouraged to allow God to transform their motives, affections, attitudes, and emotions. They were encouraged to search their souls for the thoughts and intents of the heart.

John Wesley pioneered the transformation of converts into disciples by using the same models Jesus used: large groups for teaching and small groups for relationship, discipleship, transparency and personal accountability.

A ROPE OF SAND

Adam Clark, a Methodist theologian and Biblical scholar, shared his insights as to the effectiveness and lasting fruit of the great evangelist, George Whitefield compared to the church builder, John Wesley.

It was by this means—the formation of small groups—that we have been enabled to establish permanent and holy churches all over the world. Mr. Wesley saw the necessity of this from the beginning. Mr. Whitefield, when he separated from Mr. Wesley, did not follow it.

What was the consequence? The fruit of Mr. Whitefield died with himself. Mr. Wesley's fruit remains, grows, increases, and multiplies exceedingly.

Did Mr. Whitefield see his error? He did, but not till it was too late. His people, long unused to it, would not come under this discipline.

Clark then followed with this story.

> *Whitefield met an old friend, Mr. John Pool and accosted him in the following manner: "Well, John, art thou still a Wesleyan?"*

> *Pool replied, "Yes, sir, and I thank God that I have the privilege of being in connection with him, and one of his preachers."*

> *"John," said Whitefield, "thou art in the right place. My brother Wesley acted wisely—the souls that were awakened under his ministry he joined in class (discussed in the previous section) and thus preserved the fruits of his labor. This I neglected, and my people are a rope of sand."*[205]

It must be acknowledged that at times each of us will feel that our efforts have been ineffective. Therefore, this sentiment by George Whitefield during perhaps a discouraging season cannot possibly characterize an entire ministry. However, we can surmise from Whitefield's comment that, on some level, he believed John Wesley's methods of training disciples in Societies, Classes, and Bands was indeed fruitful.

CONCLUSION

As disciples of Jesus, we are more like fire than water, created to reproduce... ourselves. It is God's deepest longing to send a revival that sweeps the Earth, ushering many millions of lost souls into His kingdom. All that He is doing in us is in preparation for this wondrous event. But unless new converts mature into Biblically literate and whole-hearted followers of Jesus, they will never fulfill their God-given destiny. It is therefore absolutely essential that the Church of Jesus ready herself to nurture and disciple the multitudes poised to enter into an eternal relationship with their Creator.

Jesus charged us, "From everyone who has been given much, much will be demanded; and from the one who has been entrusted with much, much more will be asked."[206] May we who

---

205 Lorenzen J. A Rope of Sand. Retrieved from http://onmovements.com/?p=347 on June 12, 2012.
206 John 12:48, NIV

are discerning enough to realize the critical hour facing both the church and the culture, not miss the opportunity to prepare for the many trusting spiritual children coming our way. Their future health is inexorably linked to the care and training they will most definitely need.

PRAYER FOR MAKING DISCIPLES

"Jesus, I know that You have called me to 'go and make disciples of all nations.'[207] But unless I am first Your whole-hearted follower, I am not living a life worth following. Paul wrote, 'Follow my example, as I follow the example of Christ.'[208] I pray this as well. I want to be an example of Your Christ-like character. Open no doors for me that I am not mature enough to go through. Let no one follow me if my life does not reflect Yours. Rather Lord, groom my inner man so that others would see You in me. Make me a discipler of men and women, one who is fruitful and multiplies the testimony of Your Word—all that You have so graciously given, not just to me, but to all those who are Your true disciples."

QUESTIONS FOR GROUP DISCUSSION:

1. Were you ever personally discipled by another follower of Jesus? By whom?

2. Do you take Christ's commission to make disciples of others seriously?

3. Are you presently discipling someone? If not, why not?

4. How would the church be impacted if all followers of Jesus committed to discipling others?

5. Would the commitment to disciple others fuel the move of God in a revival?

---

207 Matthew 28:19, NIV
208 1Corinthians 11:1, NIV

CHAPTER 7:
HEALING
BREACHES

Jesus said, "Blessed are the peacemakers,
for they shall be called sons of God."[209]

Loving relationships unveil the fabric of Heaven. Relational breaches break the heart of God. The root of these relational breakdowns is spiritual warfare.

Their faces are human. Their roots are supernatural. Why are relationships so important? Because if only one characteristic of God permeated all that He says and does, it would be love. God not only radiates love, He is love.[210] It is His essence!

Consequently, God embodies every healthy relational connection. Jesus lives to restore what has been lost, longs to heal what has been hurt, and died to liberate all that is bound.[211]

This restorative nature of God is stunning in itself, but what is perhaps as remarkable is that He longs for us to experience everything in His own heart. Every fruit of God's Spirit: "love, joy, peace, longsuffering, kindness, goodness, faithfulness, gentleness, [and] self-control" are Christ-like character traits He desires to impart to us.[212] We were created to display His pristine life in

---

209 Matthew 5:9, ESV
210 1John 4:8
211 Luke 4:18–20
212 Galatians 5:22–23a, NKJV

every imaginable way. As His sons and daughters, reflecting God's image is our greatest honor. Equally, misrepresenting His likeness is our greatest reproach and grieves His spirit.

Therefore we each assume both a privilege and a responsibility.

This is why seeking to restore what is lost and repair what has been fragmented is one of the primary commissions of Christ's church prior to His return. "For He [Jesus] must remain in heaven until the time for the final restoration of all things, as God promised long ago through His holy prophets."[213]

It is a breathtaking reality that Jesus is returning for "a glorious church, not having spot or wrinkle or any such thing, but that she should be holy and without blemish."[214]

He has promised us much. We, therefore, have much to prepare.

"WE" TRIUMPHS OVER "ME"

The very nature of the Godhead is an US—not a ME. "Then God said, 'Let US make man in OUR image, after OUR likeness.'"[215] God is forever inclusive. He not only incorporates intimate fellowship within the Godhead but also with those He created to be relationally connected to Him.

It is interesting to note that in Isaiah 6:8 God speaks of Himself in both a singular and plural manner. "I heard the voice of the Lord saying, 'Whom shall I send, and who will go for us?'"[216] Like the church, He is separate, yet one.

The depth of this relational connection within the Godhead can perhaps best be seen when it was broken. The lament echoed by Jesus on the cross of Calvary, "My God, My God, why have You forsaken Me?" reminds us of the profound love between Jesus and His heavenly Father.[217] At that wrenching moment His eternal fellowship with His Father was broken.

---

213 Acts 3:21, NLT
214 Ephesians 5:27, NKJV
215 Genesis 1:26a, ESV, Emphasis mine. See also Genesis 3:22 and Genesis 11:7.
216 Isaiah 6:8, ESV
217 Matthew 27:45–46, Psalm 22:1

This was perhaps God's greatest pain of all—a broken relationship. As it is for God, so it should be for us.

We have been created to care about what God cares about.

Humans differ from any other created being because only they are fashioned in the image and likeness of God. Nowhere does the Bible say that angels or animals are likewise created in God's image. Consequently, only humans may experience an intimate relationship with their Creator based on love and fellowship.

Additionally, only God and humans are capable of *incarnation*, which is "the act of taking, or being manifested in, a human body and nature."[218] When God became a man, He demonstrated the full potential of a sublime relational connection between God and mankind.[219]

Though God intentionally veils Himself, He is always highly accessible. Eager to be revealed and longing for relationship, He sets the stage for a covenant with us on His terms, for His glory, and for our good. Millions of Christians tap this relational intimacy with the invisible Creator on a daily basis. "You love Him even though you have never seen Him. Though you do not see Him now, you trust Him; and you rejoice with a glorious, inexpressible joy." [220]

We have been created for the express purpose of exploring our love potential with God, "being rooted and grounded in love, [you] may be able to comprehend with all the saints what is the width and length and depth and height—to know the love of Christ which passes knowledge; that you may be filled with all the fullness of God." We can only be filled with the fullness of God if we are filled with His essence: *love*. We must be filled with love, not just for Him, but also for one another.

Over and over again the Bible challenges us with the Mount-Everest-of-all-commands: "Love one another."[221] Not with a

---

218 "incarnation." Webster-Dictionary.net. 2009. ...Complete footnote: francisanfuso.com/awakened

219 Colossians 1:15,19

220 1Peter 1:8, NLT

221 What Does the Bible Say About Loving One ...Complete footnote: francisanfuso.com/awakened

manufactured love, but with the identical kind of love with which God has loved us. Jesus said, "A new commandment I give to you, that you love one another: just as I have loved you, you also are to love one another."[222]

WRITING PEOPLE OFF

The elephant in any room are the broken relationships. They simmer beneath the surface, aching both the heart of God and—on some level—each of us. How different the planet would be if, as Christ's followers, we would seek to repair every broken relationship.

Others have written us off. It hurts! But whom have I written off as well? What relationship is broken that God wants to heal?

The day my father died, I was glad he was gone. Though I forgave him a thousand times in my heart, it took over 40 years to completely release the hurt he caused me. But it finally came! I've had no haunting thoughts about my Dad since October of 2008.

Wanting nothing to do with someone is an expression of offense. Pride cloaks itself in self-protection, and self-protection resists the Lordship of God. I would never consider discarding or writing off any part of my natural body. As God values every person, so we should love and esteem each one as part of the body of Christ.

There are always exceptions to the rule—some individuals are really unsafe. We must not allow ourselves to become prey for predators because we ignored the caution of God's Spirit. But no one is unlovable.

With that said, many people make the mistake of living with unresolved relational breakdowns. These breaches require restoration for the fulfillment of Jesus' prayer in John 17, "that they may all be one, just as You, Father, are in Me, and I in You, that they also may be in Us, so that the world may believe that You have sent Me."[223]

---

222 John 13:34, ESV
223 John 17:21, ESV

Do we write people off because of their race or ethnicity, economic or educational background, spiritual maturity or emotional wholeness? What would Jesus do? He gave us a big hint when He provided a glimpse of the Day of Judgment, "And the King will say, 'I tell you the truth, when you did it to one of the least of these My brothers and sisters, you were doing it to Me!'"[224]

Healing breaches or breaking relationships: what will we spend our lives doing?

REVIVAL TEARS

It is of note that the word "tear" has two distinct meanings. On occasion these two words can even relate. A *tear* can be a drop that comes from eyes experiencing significant emotion, or a *tear* can happen when we "separate by violence or pull apart by force."[225] Most of us have experienced heart-breaking *teardrops* that have come from relational *tears*.

At times, we have even cried both tears of delight and devastation.

Healed relationships are designed to bring joy. As Jesus promised, "there is more joy in Heaven over one lost sinner who repents and returns to God than over ninety-nine others who are righteous and haven't strayed away,"[226]

So too, acute division leads to a broken or torn heart. This is the very heart Jesus is committed to heal. He said this when He stood in a synagogue 2,000 years ago and proclaimed, "The Spirit of the Lord is upon Me, because He has anointed Me to preach the gospel to the poor; He has sent Me to heal the brokenhearted, to proclaim liberty to the captives and recovery of sight to the blind, to set at liberty those who are oppressed..."[227]

The God who makes all things new, alone knows what a healed heart and a healthy relationship look like.[228] He is our stellar example.

---

225 "tear." Webster-Dictionary.net. 2009. ...Complete footnote: francisanfuso.com/awakened
226 Luke 15:7, NLT
227 Luke 4:18, NKJV
228 2 Corinthians 5:17

The Message Bible succinctly describes how we should relate to one another. It is a challenge worth considering.

If you've gotten anything at all out of following Christ, if his love has made any difference in your life, if being in a community of the Spirit means anything to you, if you have a heart, if you care— then do me a favor: Agree with each other, love each other, be deep-spirited friends. Don't push your way to the front; don't sweet-talk your way to the top. Put yourself aside, and help others get ahead. Don't be obsessed with getting your own advantage. Forget yourselves long enough to lend a helping hand. Think of yourselves the way Christ Jesus thought of Himself.[229]

DIVIDE AND BE CONQUERED

In order to truly represent the pure motive of a holy, humble God, we must be willing to first bow before Him. Only then can we experience oneness of heart and mind.[230] "All the believers were united in heart and mind." This marvelous oneness, characteristic of the early church, is not only possible, it is God's will.

There are no politics in Heaven. No games. No factions. No two-faces. What you see is what there is: one face, one heart, and one family. The way God intended from the beginning: birthed in humility, grounded in trust! The New Heaven and New Earth will be an exact reflection of the One who made it. This was God's plan from the beginning.

God has demonstrated His humble persona in countless ways, but most clearly in the life of Jesus. "You must have the same attitude that Christ Jesus had. Though He was God, He did not think of equality with God as something to cling to. Instead, He gave up His divine privileges; He took the humble position of a slave and was born as a human being. When He appeared in human form, He humbled Himself in obedience to God and died a criminal's death on a cross."[231]

---

229 Philippians 2:1–5, MSG
230 Acts 4:32
231 Philippians 2:5–8

We've been given a glimpse into the very makeup of God. He is—by nature—a humble servant. His character defers to others. He defines His value by giving value to others.

If God humbles Himself, it must be His explicit essence. If humility is at the core of His being, then it should be at the core of ours. We were created to be forever joined with both God, and with one another, in humble, selfless love. "God composed the body, having given greater honor to that part which lacks it, that there should be no schism in the body, but that the members should have the same care for one another."[232]

Don't bow to politics!

Don't divide and conquer!

Bow to God alone!

Only then can He conquer every dimension of our lives.

Only then can we share the joy of being like Him.

A CITY DIVIDED

Jesus assured us, "If a house is divided against itself, that house cannot stand."[233] This truth would apply to any dimension of life requiring unity in order to function and fulfill its God-given purpose.

While Scripture is clear, sound doctrine is critically important.[234] There's a BIG difference between standing my ground against sin and arrogantly standing against someone with whom I disagree. Church history records more than one perplexing struggle as Christians attempted to navigate doctrinal speed bumps.

Early in the 16th century, a doctrinal difference occurred between two great Christian reformers: German leader Martin Luther and Swiss theologian Ulrich Zwingli. Though united in their convictions on 14 points, they were unable to agree on Christ's presence during the partaking of the Lord's Supper.

---

232 1Corinthians 12:24b–25, NKJV
233 Mark 3:25, NKJV
234 2Timothy 3:16–17

Zwingli taught that communion is essentially a service of memorial and thanksgiving whereas Luther believed the communion elements were the real and actual presence of Jesus Christ, His body and blood.

Some of us might think, "Who knows and who cares?" Yet these two spiritual giants broke fellowship over this issue. In one of their meetings, the discussion literally became a shouting match. Both men later came to their senses and apologized.

These types of divisions are not uncommon throughout church history. At times, doctrinal differences caused breaches. On other occasions relational breakdowns separated those who once walked together. Such a theological division took place in the Book of Acts. "When Paul and Barnabas had a major argument and debate with them, the church appointed Paul and Barnabas and some others from among them to go up to meet with the apostles and elders in Jerusalem about this point of disagreement."[235]

Later, Paul and Barnabas faced a relational estrangement. Opposed as to whether a disciple named John Mark should accompany them on a mission trip, they parted ways. "Their disagreement over this was so sharp that they separated. Barnabas took John Mark with him."[236]

Doctrine is certainly important. However, in the book I co-authored with David Loveless, *Church Wounds*, we conducted a survey of over 1,000 participants and found that out of 26 possible categories, "doctrinal differences" was the least offensive church wound.[237] This means that, while shepherds may divide over doctrine, this problem apparently causes negligible wounds among God's sheep. Our default response may be "What do sheep know?" Perhaps they know the true meaning of what Jesus meant when He said, "By this all men will know that you are My disciples, if you have love for one another."[238]

235 Acts 15:2
236 Acts 15:39
237 Co-authored with David Loveless of Discovery Church, Orlando, Florida.
238 John 13:35, NKJV

If Jesus meant, "They'll know My disciples by their doctrine," He
would have said it. *Heart* is always higher ground than *head*. Paul,
the brilliant apostle agreed. "You think that everyone should agree
with your perfect knowledge. While knowledge may make us feel
important, it is love that really builds up the church."[239]

REPAIRING THE BREACH

From Lucifer to Laodicea, Judah to Judas, every broken
relationship becomes a breeding ground for division and
spiritual death.

Lucifer rejected God as Lord and chose himself.
He became Satan, the father of lies.[240]

The less-than-hot springs surrounding the ancient city of
Laodicea personified a tepid connection between their church
and a fiery, passionate God.[241] He longed to set them ablaze
with His deep love. They chose complacency.

The Laodiceans became lukewarm.

In the Book of Genesis, a father named Judah took advantage
of his daughter-in-law, Tamar, ignoring God's instruction to
provide and protect. This was not the first time Judah withheld
protection from someone who needed him. Previously, he had
refused to shield his younger brother Joseph, allowing him to
be sold into slavery.

Judah often failed to protect his relationships.

Finally, Judas betrayed the One who loved him most,
exchanging the eternal for the momentary.

Judas hung himself.

Each of these Bible luminaries had opportunity to mend what
was marred: the relationships in their lives. As Christ's followers
we have the privilege and, in fact, we are assigned to repair all
relational breaches. It was Jesus who, once and for all, repaired

---

239 1Corinthians 8:1b
240 John 8:44
241 Revelation 3

the breach that separated each of us from God. Now we can say with Paul the Apostle, "I am convinced that nothing can ever separate us from God's love. Neither death nor life, neither angels nor demons, neither our fears for today nor our worries about tomorrow—not even the powers of hell can separate us from God's love."[242]

Now we can claim the promise, "And your ancient ruins shall be rebuilt; you shall raise up the foundations of many generations; you shall be called the repairer of the breach, the restorer of streets to dwell in."[243] Because of this gift, we can know intimate fellowship with God and a fruitful connection with others.

Our breaches will define us—for better or worse.

They have been placed in our lives as steppingstones or stumbling blocks.

Will we perpetuate or repair them? We choose!

Those we respect most, chose wisely: Abraham with Lot, Moses with the children of Israel, Joseph with his brothers, and Jesus with His fallen creation.

Every day, it's our turn.

---

242 Romans 8:38, NLT
243 Isaiah 58:12, ESV

PRAYER FOR HEALING BREACHES

"Lord, I have been wounded by others. Though I can still feel the pain of their offense, I don't want those hurts to define my life. Nor do I want to see my life through pain. I forgive those who have hurt me. I trust that my complete healing will come and that my past hurts will not determine Your unique creation in me.

"God, I believe that my destiny is to help others heal in the same way You have healed me. Please make my healing complete. If it takes years, even decades, then so be it. Do not allow me to respond to others through my own hurts, but rather through a desire to see them healed and set free. As hurt people hurt people, so too healed people heal people. Heal me so I may be able to help heal others."

QUESTIONS FOR GROUP DISCUSSION

1. Are there relationships in your life that are presently broken? Which ones?

2. What keeps you from seeking healing for those broken relationships?

3. What would motivate you to press through those obstacles to seek healing?

4. Have you experienced breaches in relationships within your church family?

5. What steps can you take to heal broken relationships in your family, community, church, or city?

CHAPTER 8:
REPRESENTING JESUS WELL

*"I will give you a new heart and put a new spirit within you,
I will take the heart of stone out of your flesh and give you
a heart of flesh."*
Ezekiel 36:36, NKJV

I spent my young adult years far from God due, in part, to the gross misrepresentation of Jesus in my childhood. At age 15, my final prayer before heading over the cliff of willful rebellion was, "God, if you're part of what I'm experiencing, I want nothing to do with you." Even though He wasn't responsible for the misrepresentation that caused me so much pain, this was my last conversation with Him for seven long years.

My previously mentioned book, *Church Wounds*, addressed a survey of well over 1,000 participants. Results found that 86% of those surveyed had experienced church wounds, and 63% had considered not going to church again because of them. Additionally, 65% believed church wounds to be prevalent or very prevalent among their friends and family. I do not believe these findings are an anomaly but rather an accurate snapshot of a systemic dilemma ensnaring much of the Church in the Western world. Frankly, because of scandalous exposures within both the Catholic and Protestant churches, church wounds are no longer "dirty little secrets" hidden in a closet. The visceral anger of those wounded, once repressed, has now emerged with passion and spread across the landscape.

God longs to partner with us to revive His church and awaken the lost He loves so dearly. It is, of course, why He came and why we are still here. Though our task of properly representing Jesus is daunting—and at times may even seem unnatural—a supernatural anointing is available to empower us to live as Jesus lived.

GOD-BREATHED PASSIONS

We who allow Jesus to be the Lord of our lives are hard-wired to passionately care about what He cares about. Obviously, no one person can contain the vastness of God. We have each been given a share of His heart, a portion of His gifts. "It is the one and only Spirit who distributes all these gifts. He alone decides which gift each person should have."[244] We now must decide if we are willing to identify, step in to, and embrace these priceless reflections of God's Spirit.

Take a few minutes to answer the following questions:

Q. Describe what role you hope to have as God revives His people?

_____

_____

_____

_____

FOR FURTHER CONSIDERATION

As you examine what you've written, what dimensions of God-fueled burden and passion rise to the surface? You've read the book, now you can vote your heart. Which of the following areas would be your primary God-given passions? This will take some time and reflection. Ask God to show you and He will. As you examine each possibility, list them in order from #1 to #10.

Recommendation: Start by determining #1, what you are most passionate about at this point in your life, and then work your way down to #10, what you are least passionate about. All are important, but God highlights things in our hearts that are timely, not just for us but also for those around us.

Q. How would your gifts and interests be used by God to sustain a fresh, unfolding work in the God's people?

_____

_____

_____

_____

____ a. I have a passion to see Christ's followers united just as Jesus prayed.[245]

____ b. I have a passion for people to repent, see who God is, turn toward Him and away from their sins, and receive Jesus.

____ c. I have a passion to intercede for Jesus to revive His Church and awaken the lost.

____ d. I have a passion to reach the lost through preaching the gospel.

____ e. I have a passion to love, serve, and care for others.

____ f. I have a passion to mentor and coach the next generation as they follow Jesus.

____ g. I have a passion to make disciples and proclaim God's truth.

____ h. I have a passion to see relationships healed and God's people united as one.

____ i. I have a passion for God's people to truly value and esteem others.

____ j. I have a passion to represent Jesus well in every area of life, in everything I do, and everywhere I go.

---

245 John 17:21–23

In the next section, we will examine how each of these passions must emerge throughout the Body of Christ in order for a broad, sustained move of God to take place. The key word here is "sustained." It means: "continuing for an extended period or without interruption."[246] The greatest challenge to sustaining any genuine revival is to avert sabotage due to poor preparation, inappropriate responses, or insufficient commitment. Continued humility, obedience, and perseverance are necessary in order to see God's work come to completion.

CHAMPIONING THE REVIVAL

Nothing just happens. Rain doesn't fall from a clear sky. There's a cause and effect for everything. God looks for someone willing to stand in the gap for Him,[247] to separate himself from the sleepy pack, to usher in His Spirit. Scripture states, "The eyes of the Lord search the whole earth in order to strengthen those whose hearts are fully committed to him."[248]

As we speak, He's searching.

Though God invites many to be fully used by Him, precious few answer the call.[249] Any willing to receive the burden of the Lord and obey His Spirit may step into God's will for their lives. To see revival come to fruition, champions are required. These are unique vessels that fully embrace the responsibility to carry God's heart, and walk in His will for their lives.

History uncovers the essential roles assumed by champions needed to spearhead a revival. You could call them the Characteristics of a Revivalist. There is no sequence for their arrival upon the scene. Yet, the presence of each sparks a move of God to the next level.

Here are 10 dimensional roles, or God-given priorities, needing spiritual champions on a local, regional, national, and even global level. They correlate with the 10 burdens or passions listed in the

---

246 "sustained." *OxfordDictionaries.com.* 2012. ...Complete footnote: francisanfuso.com/awakened
247 Ezekiel 22:30
248 2Chronicles 16:9
249 Matthew 22:14

last section. Write the number you previously prioritized for letters "a" through "j" on the line to the left of each characteristic. (i.e. #5 for Intercession)

____ a. *Unifying* – helping unite and network the disconnected while laboring to link God's people with His gifts (John 17:21–23; Ephesians 1:10; 4:11–13; Philippians 2:2)

____ b. *Bringing a Message of Repentance* – acknowledging before a Holy God the depth of sin, modeling deep and genuine repentance for an unbelieving and rebellious church and culture (Matthew 4:17)

____ c. *Intercession* – day and night prayer for a move of God to sweep the earth, transform the church, and bring in a world wide harvest. (Isaiah 56:7; Mark 11:17; Hebrews 7:25)

____ d. *Evangelizing* – fearlessly preaching the gospel to a lost and broken generation (Ephesians 4:11; 2Timothy 4:2; 2Corinthians 10:16)

____ e. *Serving* – sacrificially serving others both within and outside the church (Matthew 20:27; 23:11; Ephesians 4:4-6; Matthew 20:28)

____ f. *Spiritual Parenting* – adopting and mentoring the next generation (1Corinthians 4:15; Malachi 4:5-6; Isaiah 9:6)

____ g. *Discipling* – meticulously teaching the Word of God to a new generation of Christ followers and carrying the message of revival to other groups or geographic regions (Matthew 28:19; Matthew 24:14; John 4:35; Acts 9:15; 13:47; Romans 1:5; 10:12-15; Revelation 5:9; 15:4)

____ h. *Restoring* – praying and working toward healing every relational breech within the Body of Christ (Isaiah 58:12)

____ i. *Encouraging* – genuinely esteeming and encouraging other individuals and churches (Philippians 2:3-8; John 3:30)

____ j. *Being a Godly Example* – representing Jesus well while modeling the fruit of God's Spirit (1Corinthians 4:9–21; 11:1)

Now consider the characteristics that burden you most, beginning with your #1 passion. Perhaps the Lord will use you to step further into these—your greatest passions—by modeling the heart of God in vital dimensions.

As you lined up your passions with actions, how would you make a growing connection between your passion and what needs to happen to encourage and sustain revival?

_____

_____

_____

_____

With this new awareness of your God-given burdens, where can you apply yourself more intentionally to further a move of God's Spirit?

_____

_____

_____

_____

Please pray and ask God to show you in which area(s) He can use you to spark a move of His Spirit. All of us have been given more than one area of passion from the Lord. As you recognize these God-given burdens in yourself and others, you will begin to see God's perfect strategy more clearly.

FOR PASTORS AND POSSIBLE LEADERS OF REVIVAL IN YOUR CHURCH / CITY

Do you know any one in your church or city that you believe is championing one of the areas discussed above? Could they play an even more significant part in the big picture by identifying this spiritual passion in their lives? If so, can they be called upon to function in one or more of the dimensions below? If you believe they can, then please write their name(s) to the left of the category.

_____ a. *Unifier* – helping unite and network the disconnected, even distrusting individuals and camps within the Body of Christ, while laboring to link God's people with His gifts and callings.

_____ b. *Messenger of Repentance* – acknowledging before a Holy God the depth of their sin, modeling deep and genuine repentance for an unbelieving and rebellious church and culture.

_____ c. *Intercessor* – crying out day and night for God to have mercy upon His wayward people.

_____ d. Evangelist – fearlessly preaching the gospel to a lost and broken generation.

_____ e. *Servant* – laying down their lives in the service of others, both within and outside the Church.

_____ f. *Spiritual Parent* – adopting the next generation and becoming spiritual parents.

_____ g. *Discipler* – meticulously teaching the Word of God to a new generation of Christ followers, and carry the anointing and message of revival to other groups or geographic regions.

_____ h. *Restorer* – believing, praying, and working toward healing every relational breakdown within the Body of Christ.

_____ i. *Encourager* – not just believing, but genuinely modeling esteeming other individuals and churches as more important than themselves.

_____ j. *Godly Example* – representing Jesus well while serving as stellar examples of being a Christ-follower.

Prayerfully consider sharing the names you have written above with spiritual leaders in your own life, as well as with those individuals themselves.

THE LAST STAND

If you know your unique role in ushering God's presence in greater measure, are you committed to it? One verse is clear: "Patient endurance is what you need now, so that you will continue to do God's will. Then you will receive all that He has promised."[250]

Every genuine follower of Jesus Christ must come to the point where he or she is either "all in," or at least admits, "Unless I yield to God's Spirit, I will not become all God intended me to be." We must stop nibbling around the edges. We must stop enabling deceptive desires. We must stop allowing half-baked commitments to steal ultimate destinies. This is our best shot at fulfilling the will of God for our lives. We accept that this unprecedented opportunity may be our last stand and may not come again.

None of us want to be a General Custer and die for nothing— making a last stand at the wrong time, in an ill-advised place, for a faulty reason. We fast and pray, imploring God to keep us from succumbing to such a great deception.[251]

Much will be lost if we refuse to fully surrender to what we know is God's will. Likewise, much will be gained if we obey with complete abandon.

So, the question must be asked: do we truly ache to be like Jesus, to lay it all down for the One who has loved us most? The great God of the universe allowed His body to be brutally mutilated and His Spirit separated from His heavenly Father for us. He did this to demonstrate that there is nothing He would not do for us and for our good. May we make this same choice today!

---

250 Hebrews 10:36, NLT
251 Psalm 19:13

PRAYER FOR REPRESENTING JESUS WELL

"Lord, I have been most hurt by others when they name Your name but badly misrepresent You. As it was the last thing I wanted done to me, it is now the last thing I would ever want to do to others. So, please forgive me when I don't walk the talk or live the life I know You have created me to live.

"Thank You for never giving up on me even when I give up on myself. I know that it is only by Your grace and with Your wisdom and power that I can in the future truly represent You well. This would be the greatest answer to prayer I could ever receive. Amen!"

QUESTIONS FOR GROUP DISCUSSION

1. On a scale of 1 to 10, with 10 being high, how would you rate yourself in representing Jesus well to others? Keep in mind that though all of us fall short, He has promised us grace to represent Him well.

2. Are there areas in your life that you live one way publically and another way in private?

3. Share with others in your group or a close friend the unique passion(s) that Christ has placed within you (pages 71 and 72). If you are uncertain, ask someone who knows you well what they believe is your passion.

4. Why do you believe you are called to these?

5. What practical steps can you take in order to see these much-needed dimensions of spiritual passion become established in your life, church, and city?

CHAPTER 9: ESTEEMING OTHERS FIRST

Throughout history, a man's word has been his bond. A verbal commitment and handshake have been enough to seal a deal. For if a man shakes your hand and continues to live in the same community, he stakes his honor and reputation. Even more telling are a person's last words.

One of Jesus' final requests to His Father was not merely that His followers would be one with Him, but that they would be one with each other. He even went so far as to declare that the unified Body of Christ on Earth would compel others to believe in Him: "that they all may be one, as You, Father, are in Me, and I in You; that they also may be one in Us, that the world may believe that You sent Me."[252]

How important is this concept? It's shocking to think that Jesus proclaimed that it would determine whether or not the world believed that God the Father sent Him. Our choice to fully love one another as He intended could be the very stepping-stone for someone else's belief.

Even within the natural order, the need for oneness is compelling. A disunited body is called dysfunctional. In contrast, we give medals and trophies to individuals whose body parts are so developed and finely tuned that they flow as one.

In the spirit realm, oneness or unity is the ultimate indication of spiritual health as well. Whether within a marriage, a family, a team, a company, or a church, the way in which we join together will reflect our relationship with Christ.

Harmony among Christ's followers ought to convince the unbelieving world that we truly belong to Him. It should testify to real love and its influence. Jesus said, "By this all people will know that you are my disciples, if you have love for one another."[253] Why should anyone believe we actually have a relationship with the God Who is love if we refuse to genuinely love one another?

The answer is they won't!

The fact is that our commitment to be one with other followers of Jesus by loving them as He's asked is perhaps the primary stamp of authenticity that draws others to Jesus. My inability to love and accept the person I *know* will directly undermine my ability to love the person I *don't yet know*.

Christ's prayer for oneness will be answered before His return. Our call is to value every vital member of His Body, from the head down.

WHO'S GOT YOUR BACK?

Is there any part of your body that you would consider expendable? Ever stub a toe? Cut a finger? Get a fleck in your eye? You'll be hopping, squeezing, and yelling, "Can you see it? Can you see it?" In that red-alert moment, other parts of your body rush to the aid of the injured member. It doesn't have to be bleeding or blinding to get your full attention. Except for my hair and nails, don't mess with any part of me. If it's attached to me, I'm attached to it.

Wouldn't this principle apply to the less visible parts of my body as well? Are they any less important? My heart, lungs, liver, and kidneys may be hidden, but I cannot live without them. I may never have given them a hug, or paid any attention to them

---

253 John 13:35, NKJV

whatsoever, but if one of my life-giving organs conks out, I'll know about it in a heartbeat. In that 9-1-1 instant, every other member of my stricken body will do whatever it can to get the failed organ up and running again.

Just as a safety net of mutual assistance works within our natural body, the same principle applies to our spiritual body. "The body we're talking about is Christ's body of chosen people. Each of us finds our meaning and function as a part of his body. But as a chopped-off finger or cut-off toe we wouldn't amount to much, would we? So since we find ourselves fashioned into all these excellently formed and marvelously functioning parts in Christ's body, let's just go ahead and be what we were made to be, without enviously or pridefully comparing ourselves with each other, or trying to be something we aren't."[254] As our natural bodies include only significant members, so too does Christ's spiritual Body.

Do we live with this conscious sense of our need for others? We should! It is reality! In a very real sense, one member's failure affects all. Within the healthcare industry, destructive behaviors like smoking, drug or alcohol abuse, or overeating, pose a threat not just to the individual, but also to the spiritual, social and economic wellbeing of an entire community. My failing brakes would jeopardize not only the wheels, but also the whole car, even those in my path.

The repercussions of good and bad behavior can be noted from the beginning of time. Adam and Eve's sin still impacts me today. So too does the second Adam's (Jesus') sacrifice save me. Likewise, my rebellion or obedience can curse or bless the next generation. We have painfully witnessed how the moral failure of a high-profile Christian affects all Christ-followers. We have also seen changed lives mentored and cared for by no-name believers.

Athletes function at the highest level because each member of his or her body flows harmoniously together. In contrast, a disabled person struggles with body parts that refuse to cooperate. Such will be the fate of Christ's Body if it refuses to recognize the value of its members.

Either we willingly submit and support one another in order to accomplish a greater goal than any individual member could achieve, or our disunity becomes our indefensible epitaph.

PASTORS: AN ENDANGERED SPECIES

What would happen if a pastor in your city was murdered and his body was dumped at the steps of City Hall? Would anyone care? You bet they would! At that paradigm-shifting moment, if a senior leader from one of the area churches called a meeting of all pastors, interest would pique and schedules would change. A radical alteration would dramatically transform our behavior.

Now, let's say within a few days of the first homicide a second pastor was brutally killed and his body likewise discarded. If another meeting of pastors was called, I doubt if a single pastor would fail to attend. Overnight the immediate need of the city's spiritual leaders would trump all other meetings and appointments. Fervent prayers would be prayed. Commitments would be made. Offerings would be taken. A new resolve to uphold and protect one another would universally be applauded and agreed upon.

While some might consider this violent assault against Christians a far-fetched scenario, it isn't. Frankly, it's happened throughout history and is happening in many nations around the world. Right now, across America, surveys have shown pastors and spiritual leaders are under attack like never before. Consider these chilling statistics:[255, 256]

- Fifteen hundred pastors leave the ministry each month due to moral failure, spiritual burnout, or contention in their churches.

- Four thousand new churches open each year, but over seven thousand established churches close.

- Fifty percent of pastors' marriages end in divorce.

255 Krejcir RJ. Statistics on Pastors. Schaeffer Institute. ...Complete footnote: francisanfuso.com/awakened
256 Oliver GJ. Church Initiatives. The Center for ...Complete footnote: francisanfuso.com/awakened

- Fifty percent of pastors are so discouraged, they would leave the ministry if they could, but have no other way to make a living.

- Eighty percent of seminary and Bible school graduates who enter the ministry leave the ministry within the first five years.

- Eighty percent of pastors' spouses wish their spouse would choose another profession.

- The majority of pastor's wives surveyed said that the most destructive event that has occurred in their marriage and family was the day they entered the ministry.

- Seventy percent of pastors constantly fight depression.

Do we really need more data before we act to stem the tide of dissipation among church leaders? To wait for a more alarming report will likely render our response too little, too late.

Isolated for too long, even the best leader tends to self-destruct. The Bible repeatedly confirms the inherent dangers of relational detachment and disconnection. "It's not good for man to be alone."[257] And "pity the man who falls and has no-one to help him up!"[258] If there was ever a person who shouldn't be forsaken or left alone, it's a spiritual leader.

ESTEEMING OTHERS FIRST

I once went to a conference for pastors in which the main speaker's message was entitled "How To Deal With the Joy-Suckers In Your Church." At one point in his talk, this well-known, highly respected man of God even went so far as to say, "There's no greater joy than doing the funeral of a joy-sucker."

The room erupted in laughter. My heart sank.

Though I knew the speaker meant to encourage pastors besieged with criticism, this perspective isn't helpful or Biblical. I find no eternal value in regarding those I've been graced to care for as "joy-suckers" no matter how irritating they might be. Certainly

---

257 Genesis 2:18
258 Ecclesiastes 4:10

the mandate of Jesus: "Do to others as you would have them do to you,"[259] would provide incentive enough to view everyone with extreme grace.

If, for whatever reason, my heart was still unwilling to offer compassion to all, then I should probably consider the scriptural guarantee, "you reap whatever you sow."[261] The math is simple: if I have a disparaging view of others, I shouldn't be surprised if they have the same of me. If, on the other hand, I absorb the criticism that has merit and deflect that which has none, God's love will help me cover a multitude of hurtful attitudes and words toward me.

We must not respond like the world when we are attacked. Mimicking our cynical, self-protecting culture will only breed a spirit of rejection and elitism. If this condescending attitude infects the Church, we will act no different than the accuser in Revelation 12:10, who merely seeks to divide Christ's Body.

I have tried to live this way for many years, and found that my gentle answer deflects most anger sent my way.[261] As one who has been showered with a lifetime of undeserved mercy, I want God's mercy to triumph over any judgmental attitude the enemy may use to seduce me.[262] Isn't that what Jesus did for us? He covered our foolish words, attitudes, and lives with forgiveness, mercy, and love. He's still doing it. "God blesses those who are merciful, for they will be shown mercy."[263]

Of all the people I have ever known, I believe I deserve the least mercy. If anyone was guilty of sucking joy from innocent victims, it was I. As an adamant in-your-face atheist, I would laugh aloud and mock my saintly mother as she bowed her head and prayed over her food. In spite of my incredibly hurtful behavior, my long-suffering Mom modeled the heart of our Heavenly Father who longs to see "all people to be saved and to come to the knowledge

---

259 Luke 6:31, NIV
260 Galatians 6:7, NRSV
261 Proverbs 15:1
262 James 2:13
263 Matthew 5:7, NLT

of the truth."[264] Ultimately, her prayers won out, and I was awakened out of my deception.

The united Godhead, Father, Son, and Holy Spirit always models unity, mercy, and selfless, vulnerable love. It cost God everything to come to Earth; it will cost us much to represent Him properly. Only when everyone is looked *up to*, does no one feel looked *down upon*. The Bible affirms this premiere principle when it charges us, "Do nothing from rivalry or conceit, but in humility count others more significant than yourselves."[265] This is not some pie-in-the-sky concept; it's God's directive. Therefore, it must be ours as well.

"ESTEEMING OTHERS FIRST" COMMITMENT

What would happen to your city if every genuine follower of Jesus modeled Godhead unity, esteeming others first, and made the following commitment? Perhaps the outpouring of God's Spirit we are praying and believing for.

- *I commit* to build the Kingdom of God, not my own kingdom. I will never fulfill my destiny and become the person God created me to be without being vitally connected in love to other members and leaders within Christ's Body in my city.

  Jesus said, "that they all may be one, as You, Father, are in Me, and I in You; that they also may be one in Us, that the world may believe that You sent Me."[266]

- *I commit* to wholeheartedly model the love of God toward others. Jesus said, "By this all people will know that you are my disciples, if you have love for one another."[267]

- *I commit* to esteem others as more important than myself because God desires me to pray for and value the success of others as a greater goal than my own success.

  "Do nothing from rivalry or conceit, but in humility count others more significant than yourselves."[268]

---

264 1Timothy 2:4, ESV
265 Philippians 2:3, ESV
266 John 17:21
267 John 13:35
268 Philippians 2:3

- *I commit* to encourage pastors and other spiritual leaders in any way possible.

"Do not withhold good from those to whom it is due, when it is in your power to do it."[269]

Unless we care about what Jesus cares about, we will find it is utterly impossible to represent Him well.

☐ Yes, I am willing to make this "Esteeming Others First" Commitment.

PRAYER FOR ESTEEMING OTHERS FIRST

"Lord Jesus, You know I have put myself first on more occasions than I can count. It has never satisfied me, and I know it has never pleased You. But Your Word is clear. You have opened my eyes to see that one of my chief goals in life is to esteem others as more important than myself. It is a cherished role and lofty goal, but with Your help—doable! So, I ask for the grace I need each day to not bow to selfish preferences, but to Your perfect will for my life. In Your name, Amen!"

QUESTIONS FOR GROUP DISCUSSION

1. What relationship(s) do you currently have in which you feel someone "has your back"? If you don't have any, why not?
2. On a scale of 1 to 10, with 10 being high, how would you rate yourself in esteeming others first? Why?
3. What specifically hinders you from fully esteeming and valuing others?
4. What practical step(s) can you take to esteem others as more important than yourself?
5. Share one situation when you esteemed someone as more important than yourself. What impact did it have on that person? What impact did it have on you?

---

269 Proverbs 3:27, ESV

LEADER: ARE YOU SAFE?

One of the most vulnerable positions in the Body of Christ is a Christian leader seeking to further the Kingdom of God. Whether, a pastor, ministry head, civic or business leader, the bulls-eye on each of their lives is real, and requires focused prayer in order for them to be protected. Like Moses, they need an Aaron and Hur to come along side in intercession so that their lives are protected and Kingdom advances can be made. Though breaches have at times formed between leaders and intercessors preventing them from functioning together as God ordained, when humble, mutually respectful relationships are formed, they provide a magnificent, protective prayer shield. This will require significant confidentiality, transparency, and humility between leaders and intercessors, but when flowing as God intended, the body of Christ has been given a spiritual immune system, provided the safeguards needed for its protection.

We also realize that when intercessors function in their God-given stewardship, they are likewise vulnerable to the attack of the enemy. They too need a prayer shield.

A strategic intercession model was developed in Africa where both the leader and intercessor are covered with prayer, increasing their effectiveness and protection.

The basic structure is simple yet very effective. Twelve intercessors form the ideal team.

- Each intercessor takes one day of the week to fast and pray for a leader.

- Two additional intercessors cover in prayer each of these intercessors as they fast and pray.

- Alternate intercessors form part of the team and can fill in slots as needed.

Using this innovative approach, we have seen God work in extraordinary ways, expanding His Kingdom as well as bringing unity between leaders and intercessors.

To learn more about this model check out:
www.intercessorsworkshop.org

APPENDIX

INTERCESSORY PETITIONS

Listed below are ten intercessory petitions helpful in galvanizing prayer for key leaders in the church in your city and region. These are the pivotal battleground arenas. If they can be secured first in Heaven and then on Earth, God will release His grace and favor. Resist forming your own timeframe or expectations. The times, seasons, and results are always in the safe hands of the God who cares infinitely more than we do.

Trust God! Obey Him! Enjoy the ride! Believe that love never fails![270]

1. Pray for protection for your local church pastor and his family. Petition God to protect them from spiritual deception, relational breakdown, or physical and financial mishap that will undermine what He has intended for their precious lives. Ask God to grant your local church pastor the wisdom, grace, humility, and sensitivity to the Holy Spirit necessary in this critical hour.

2. Pray for protection for the pastors and leaders of churches in your region. Petition God to protect them from spiritual deception, relational breakdown, or physical and financial mishap that will undermine His intension for their precious lives. In particular, pray protection over specific leaders whom you believe are essential in order for an outpouring of God's Spirit to come to your region.

3. Pray for an unprecedented spirit of unity amongst the pastors and leaders of churches in your region.

4. Pray for God's gift of repentance to overtake Christian leaders, congregations, and all Christ followers throughout your region.

---

270 1Corinthians 13:8

5. Pray for the church to be revived and the lost to be awakened. Ask God to quicken hearts to rely on prayer as the best hope for their loved ones.

6. Pray for a spirit of selfless service to come upon multitudes of Christ-followers in this region during this coming season.

7. Pray for a mighty harvest of young people to sweep across this region rescuing and awakening multitudes to follow Jesus.

8. Pray for the next move of God to make disciples, whole-hearted followers of Jesus, not merely converts or carnal Christians.

9. Pray for protection from the many dangers inherent to revival such as spiritual deception, excess or extremism, division by offenses, jealousies and insecurities. Ask God for healing, covered by the blood of Jesus Christ, between church leaders and congregations.

10. Pray for healing of past breaches in relationships between churches, leaders, and believers. May no attitudes of offense and division remain.

"AWAKENED" SMALL GROUPS

This book and accompanying video may be used in a ten-week small group format. Here is the recommended small group structure and weekly assignments.

Review Video: Each small group participant should **view the designated segment of the "AWAKENED" video at www. revivalstories.org/awakened** before reading the section of "AWAKENED" assigned. Additionally, we recommend this video segment be shown during the small group, prior to discussion.

Group Discussion: At the end of each of the nine chapters in this book there are questions to discuss.

Fellowship, Worship, and Prayer: May precede or follow the discussion.

The Ten Weekly Assignments for small groups are as follows:

WEEK 1 – Read the Foreword, Introduction, Prologue
and Filming in Wales
VIEW VIDEO PART 1 – Introduction

WEEK 2 – Read Chapter 1
VIEW VIDEO PART 2 – Desperate Times
Discuss Questions at the end of Chapter 1

WEEK 3 – Read Chapter 2
VIEW VIDEO PART 3 – Life and Death Prayers
Discuss Questions at the end of Chapter 2

WEEK 4 – Read Chapter 3
VIEW VIDEO PART 4 – Gift of Repentance
Discuss Questions at the end of Chapter 3

WEEK 5 – Read Chapter 4
VIEW VIDEO PART 5 – Supernatural Surprises
Discuss Questions at the end of Chapter 4

WEEK 6 – Read Chapter 5
VIEW VIDEO PART 6 – Selfless Serving
Discuss Questions at the end of Chapter 5

WEEK 7 – Read Chapter 6
VIEW VIDEO PART 7 – Making Disciples
Discuss Questions at the end of Chapter 6

WEEK 8 – Read Chapter 7
VIEW VIDEO PART 8 – Healing Breaches
Discuss Questions at the end of Chapter 7

WEEK 9 – Read Chapter 8
VIEW VIDEO PART 9 – Representing Jesus Well
Discuss Questions at the end of Chapter 8

WEEK 10 – Read Chapter 9
VIEW VIDEO PART 10 – Esteeming Others First
Discuss Questions at the end of Chapter 9

RECOMMENDED BOOKS
OTHER TITLES BY FRANCIS ANFUSO

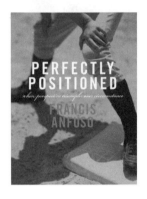

Perfectly Positioned—
When Perspective Triumphs Over Circumstance*
Do you wish God had written a different script for you? Do you see your life as an exquisite feast or burnt toast? Are you eating and enjoying every bite or is it boring, bland and predictable? Are you filled with regret and shame or hope and healing? Our lives begin to be truly transformed when we stop asking God to change our circumstances, and allow Him to change our perspective! Behind every challenging situation there is a loving God whose victorious perspective is far greater than the trials we face. God's will is that we would embrace the life He has given us, instead of wishing for what does not exist and would not satisfy even if it did. If you have come to the realization that you have fished all night and caught nothing, it is not an accident. Keep fishing! God has perfectly positioned you to read this book. The breakthrough you have been longing for is just ahead!

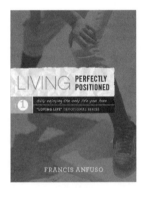

Living Perfectly Positioned—
"Loving Life" Devotional Series
This book could be called: "The Greatest Hits of Perfectly Positioned." The best of the best revelations are in bite-size, one-a-day pieces. Instead of wishing you had a different script for your life, God can renew your mind to enjoy the only life you have. By changing your perspective, you will see your life changed! God's will is that we would embrace the life He has given us, instead of wishing for what does not exist and would not satisfy even if it did. If you have come to the realization that you have fished all night and caught nothing, it's not an accident. Keep fishing! God has perfectly positioned you to read this book. The breakthrough you have been longing for is just ahead!

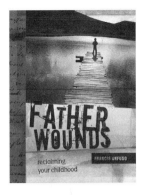

Father Wounds—Reclaiming Your Childhood*

As an abandoned and abused son, my soul suffered long-term destruction. But my wounded heart was exactly what God wanted to heal and restore. I discovered God is the Father I always wanted. He's the perfect Dad I needed all along. God can help you forgive the parent who hurt you. He wants to heal you completely and use you mightily in the lives of others! Today is the day to step into the wholeness and destiny God has for His children! (Find video clips online at rockspots.tv)

2029—The Church of the Future*

You can comprehend the future if you study the past and discern the present. God is not hiding what is about to happen. He longs to reveal it to us. In 1989, Francis Anfuso wrote We've Got a Future—The 21st Century Church. Now, two decades after its release, the book reads like a detailed depiction of today's church. But the story is far from finished. This next volume details what is about to unfold—where the church must go, and the significant role you can play. 2029 is a glimpse into our future. A taste of what will shortly come to pass. Now is not the time for the Church to shrink back and recoil as the battle rages. Instead, we are approaching our finest hour.

Church Wounds—
Francis Anfuso and David Loveless*

Our wounds don't have to disable us. They're meant to be a doorway into the restored life God always intended. God wants to heal us, if we want to be. For God to free us, we must allow Him to touch our pain. Church Wounds examines the most common hurts inflicted by Christians on Christians: hypocrisy, judgmentalism, leader insensitivities, and abuse, plus many more. Read the stories of those who were not just hurt—but healed; and then experience the healing yourself.

*Book available in MP3, read by author
Printed books and MP3's by Francis Anfuso may be purchased at francisanfuso.com

NUMB

We all fight numbness and its long-term effect. Unless our daily reality is greater than our inner fantasy, we'll wander from one reality-replacement to another. When we forget what we know—we forfeit who we are.

Everything God does is designed to lead us into intimacy with Him—to set us free from boredom, loneliness, and self-absorbed distractions. He loves us enough to allow us to be satisfied with only Himself.

Identity / Destiny Prayer Journal

The first step in fulfilling your destiny is finding your identity, and only God knows the answer to this question. My true identity is who He created me to be. My ultimate destiny is what He has called me to do. In our natural life we will only see what we are willing to focus upon. But…"In prayer there is a connection between what God does and what you do." Matthew 6:14 (MSG) It is in prayer that God helps us understand Him in fresh ways and deeper levels. We connect with Him and He unlocks His kingdom within us. Inside this 40-Day Prayer Journal you will examine areas of life that will call for new focus and connected prayer. In so doing, you will experience the endlessly delightful relationship He promises.

revivalstories.org

Why do we need a revival? Because a revival does what only God can do. Revival is when God springs a convicting surprise on His creation — it's when Jesus is so lifted up, He draws multitudes to Himself. At revivalstories.org, you can access powerful videos describing some of the greatest revival moments throughout history. From the Great Awakenings to the great evangelists and revivalists, revival stories unlocks the heartbeat of the why and how of revivals. When a generation gets so desperate for Jesus to transform their culture that Christians finally humble themselves, and cry out in desperation for God to intervene.